Making Black Los Angeles

Making Black Los Angeles

Class, Gender, and Community, 1850–1917

Marne L. Campbell

The University of North Carolina Press *Chapel Hill*

Set in Espinosa Nova and Alegreya Sans by Westchester Publishing Services

Manufactured in the United States of America

The University of North Carolina Press has been a member of the Green Press Initiative since 2003.

Library of Congress Cataloging-in-Publication Data

Names: Campbell, Marne L.

Title: Making black Los Angeles : class, gender, and community, 1850–1917 / Marne L. Campbell.

Description: Chapel Hill : University of North Carolina Press, [2016] | Includes bibliographical references and index.

Identifiers: LCCN 2016008486 | ISBN 9781469629261 (cloth : alk. paper) | ISBN 9781469629278 (pbk : alk. paper) | ISBN 9781469629285 (ebook)

Subjects: LCSH: African Americans—California—Los Angeles—Social conditions—19th century. | African Americans—California—Los Angeles—Social conditions—20th century. | Community life—California—Los Angeles—History—19th century. | Community life—California—Los Angeles—History—20th century. | Los Angeles (Calif.)—Race relations—History—19th century. | Los Angeles (Calif.)—Race relations—History—20th century.

Classification: LCC F869.L89 N3265 2016 | DDC 305.8009794/9409034—dc23 LC record available at http://lccn.loc.gov/2016008486

Cover illustration: Family portrait, Los Angeles, ca. 1918 (Security Pacific Bank Collection, Los Angeles Public Library, #00048301).

Frontis: Lishey Family, 1910, Watts, California. Ruth (holding a violin), Lettie, Oliver, Robert, and Gladys. Los Angeles Public Library, Shades of L.A. Collection.

Portions of this book have been published as: "African American Women, Wealth Accumulations, and Social Welfare Activism in 19th Century Los Angeles," *Journal of African American History* 97, no. 4 (Fall 2012); and "The Newest Religious Sect Has Started in Los Angeles: Race, Class, Ethnicity, and the Origins of the Pentecostal Movement, 1906–1913," *Journal of African American History* 95 no. 1 (Fall 2009).

For my parents, Isaac and Diana Campbell.
I know you're smiling down on me from heaven.

Contents

Illustrations

Acknowledgments

This project started out as something completely different, but has ended as something I am truly proud of, and there are so many people who have helped me get through it.

When I was an undergraduate student at UCLA, I was introduced to Brenda E. Stevenson. She was the only faculty member at the time who was working on black women, and that's what I was mostly interested in studying. I went into the Interdepartmental Program in Afro-American Studies for my master's degree, and focused on slave women. I also applied to, and was accepted, by the Department of History at UCLA to continue my research, but because of certain situations, I decided to change my topic. While I thought I was going to be a strict slavery scholar, Brenda encouraged me to do this research, and has taught me to do (I think) very good research. Brenda, thank you so much for believing in me, especially when I wanted to give up, and give in.

I want to thank all of the people at UCLA who helped me along the way, from undergraduate to graduate school in both Afro-American Studies and History. First, the faculty and staff who have been there for me: In Afro-American Studies (back then), Valerie Smith, Richard Yarborough, Darnell Hunt, Sid Lemelle, Paul Von Blum, Mark Sawyer, Jan Freeman, Itibari Zulu, and Veronica Benson were very supportive of me. In the Department of History thanks to Steve Aron and Kevin Terraciano, who both gave constructive feedback on this project. In addition, Brenda Stevenson and Richard Yarborough were so helpful, along with other faculty and staff like John Lasslett, Muriel McClendon, Ron Mellor, Ruth Bloch, Richard Weiss, Gary B. Nash, and Nancy Dennis. I also want to thank the Institute of American Cultures, the Ralph J. Bunche Center for African American Studies (CAAS, when I was an undergrad), and the UCLA Graduate Division for supporting my research.

I have had tremendous support from staff at several archives, including the Seaver Center for Western History research, the Autry Museum of Western History, the California State Library and the California State Archive, the Los Angeles Public Library, and UCLA Library's department of Special Collections. I have also had generous support from the

University of California President's Office as a President's Postdoctoral Fellow, and the Huntington Library. I thank all of the staff at each of these institutions, especially Kimberly Adkinson at the UC Office of the President, and Jaeda Snow and Alison Monheim at the Huntington Library.

My family has been very supportive of this endeavor, even though I lost my mother in 1999 and my father in 2007. I love and miss you both so very much. Not a day goes by that I don't think about you. Thanks to my big brother, Isaac Campbell III. You were there for me, Isaac, when times were roughest. I love you so much! DeShaun Davis, I'm pretty sure you set the standard for patience. Thank you. And my fictive kin: Emma and James Cones—thank you for allowing me to be part of your family. Emma, you are the best little sister anyone could ask for! You really do make my life bright! Brenda Stevenson you have been supportive of me and of my work above and beyond measure. I think it's safe to say that we've been through a lot together, and through it all, you have been my mentor, my friend, and my family. I have learned so much from you, and because of you, I am a better person and scholar. I hope this work makes you proud, but mostly, I hope it reflects the kind of training you have given me. Also, Karen and Lee Eckes, Robin Reinhard, the Clair family, Jonesy, Skyler Harris, Michelle Schultz, Christopher "Romeo" Romero, Kimberly "Mimi" Romero, and Jeff Reinhard. You all have helped me through some really rough times, and through it all, you kept encouraging me to pursue this project. Thank you.

I have several colleagues who have been supportive of me at different stages of this project. First, I want to thank my LMU colleagues—Angela James, Adilifu Nama, and Brad Stone in African American Studies; Traci Voyles, Sina Kramer, and Stella Oh in Women's Studies; and Karen Mary Davalos in Chicana/o Studies. Two of my other colleagues in Chicana/o Studies, Eliza Rodriguez y Gibson and Yvette Saavedra (#anythingforsaavedra), have become my really close friends, and I am so grateful to have you in my life. Thank you so much for your support, your friendship, and your truly valuable feedback. Thanks to my colleagues and former colleagues from LMU: Dorothea Herreiner, Linh Hua, Maria Valenzuela, Jane Yamashiro, Deanna Cooke, Rae Linda Brown, Abbie Robinson-Armstrong, Danielle Borgia, Deena Gonzalez, and Edward Park. Liz Faulkner has been particularly supportive. And my good friend and colleague Heather Tarleton—it has been absolutely wonderful having a writing partner during this final stretch.

You are always encouraging, and I don't think you know how much your positive attitude has helped me.

I also have several good friends to thank. Some are colleagues, but they have been my friends beyond work. Jessica Millward—thank you for asking all the right questions, checking in when I needed, and knowing when I needed to keep my head down. It's been a great (almost) two decades, my friend. Clarence Lang—thank you for pushing me to keep at it. I know it didn't seem like it at times, but I always heard, and I always listened. Thanks Eboni Stevens, Janique "Jammie" Dunn, Chloe Kipnis, Leonardo Zuniga, LaShawn Witt, Shaneé Somerville, and Hooman Rahimizadeh. Special thanks to Lovell "Lovey" Seville, I know you are resting peacefully, and that heaven is a happier place with you in it, even though we miss you down here.

Thanks also to several mentors and other colleagues who have given me valuable feedback and moral support: Randal Jelks, the Association of Black Women's Historians (ABWH), Francille Rusan Wilson, Tiffany M. Gill, Yohuru Williams, and Pablo Miguel Sierra Silva. I owe a special thanks to V. P. Franklin, who was my mentor at UC Riverside. You and Ed (Collins) took very good care of me beyond the work, while pushing me all the while. Thank you both for all of the support. I want to thank several of my students who were very supportive: Juliet Doris, Alexis Hunley, Christopher Williams, Briana Cook, Kayla Hampton, Kendra Dawson, Kaelyn Sabal-Wilson, and Robyn Rouzan. I especially want to thank my undergraduate research assistants at LMU Nadia Kelifa, Toni Richardson, Starr Joseph, Zoe Jackson, Aaliyah Jordan, Jasmine Harris, and Justine Dominguez. #amazing!

Making Black Los Angeles

Introduction

At the beginning of the twentieth century, two of the most prominent African American leaders, W. E. B. Du Bois and Booker T. Washington, visited California. Washington visited twice, in 1903 and in 1914. Du Bois traveled to the state in 1913, and wrote extensively about Los Angeles in his *Crisis Magazine*'s volume entitled, "Colored California." He believed that the city offered more to African Americans than any other region of the country. Du Bois wrote, "One never forgets Los Angeles and Pasadena: the sensuous beauty of roses and orange blossoms, the air and the sunlight and the hospitality of all its races linger on."[1]

Du Bois described Los Angeles as possessing "sensuous beauty," with wonderful weather and climate that extended to its inhabitants. He noted the African American community's efforts in the local economy, their beautiful houses, and the ways in which they worked with other communities of color. Du Bois also believed black Angelenos worked well with one another to create opportunities for themselves and for their community as a whole. African Americans in Los Angeles, Du Bois concluded, challenged their oppressive circumstances and overcame adversity better than any other city in California.[2]

Booker T. Washington also toured California, making his second trip a year after Du Bois's visit. Unlike Du Bois, however, Washington did not publish his observations about Los Angeles or the west. Washington visited with wealthy Black Angelenos, spoke at several churches, addressed the "colored" YMCA, several women's clubs, and attended dinner with most of the people who hosted W. E. B. Du Bois one year before.[3]

During both of his visits to Los Angeles, Washington was impressed with the accomplishments of African Americans and the treatment he received. He appreciated the ways in which black Angelenos managed their own businesses, their churches, and their ability to secure property. Perhaps the only thing he was more impressed by was the idle gossip of one dinner party at the home of one of the wealthiest African Americans in the west, Robert C. Owens, who also hosted W. E. B. Du Bois. Washington said, "It seems he made a perfect fool of himself by trying to snub everybody."[4] He also said that black Angelenos would not be inviting Du Bois for a return visit, and that none of them had anything positive to say about his adversary. Washington concluded that the best way to compete with Du Bois was to let him meet people all over the country.[5]

Both Du Bois and Washington envisioned equality for African Americans. But they had very different ideas about the ways in which African Americans could achieve it. For Washington, success was achieved through hard work, economic independence, and self-sufficiency. Du Bois, on the other hand, advocated attaining civil rights, educating the youth, and securing the right to vote. Many African Americans at the beginning of the twentieth century embraced these ideas, either by supporting agricultural and industrial training at schools like Washington's Tuskegee Institute, or by joining political organizations such as the National Association for the Advancement of Colored People (NAACP), co-founded by Du Bois. Others utilized a combination of ideas from both.

Both Booker T. Washington and W. E. B. Du Bois were towering figures, and each influenced Black Angelenos at the turn of the twentieth century. While Du Bois romanticized the status of African Americans throughout the city, he really only focused on the elite sectors of the community, thereby concluding that life was indeed better in Los Angeles and California than other American cities. Washington, on the other hand, was hoping to raise money for, and promote Tuskegee Institute. While he maintained a close relationship with many of the black elite, Washington's message was a more natural fit for the black working class in Los Angeles, and throughout the West. African Americans also drew from other sources of black leadership, such as Marcus Garvey's United Negro Improvement Association (UNIA).

Yet local men and women were also crucial to Los Angeles's black community. Leaders like Charlotta Bass and Jefferson Edmonds owned and operated the city's black newspapers. William J. Seymour led the multiethnic, multiracial Azusa Street Revival. Joseph and Elizabeth Young were both members of several clubs and organizations such as the YMCA and the California State Association of Colored Women, respectively. Georgia Robinson became the first black policewoman in America in 1919, and then became the first black social worker in Los Angeles.[6]

The long history of leadership drawn from the community of black Angelenos can be traced to the first families of African descent. Those who arrived in Los Angeles at the beginning of the twentieth century reaped the benefits of achievements made by African Americans since the 1850s. During the late nineteenth century African Americans fought for and won access to housing and public education, in addition to testimony and voting rights. By the time Washington and Du Bois arrived, black Angelenos had already made significant gains, even though they had not attained full equality.

Most histories of black Los Angeles tend to overlook the two visits by Washington, even as they emphasize Du Bois's conclusions. By the time he arrived in California, Du Bois already had published two major studies on race relations and the status of African Americans. He, perhaps more than anyone else, was equipped with the tools to analyze the status of African Americans in this "new" century. In his 1899 book, *The Philadelphia Negro*, Du Bois investigated the state of urban African Americans at the turn of the century in this eastern city. Four years later, Du Bois published *The Souls of Black Folk* (1903), a collection of essays from his own experience in the American South. Both were sociological studies of African American communities that confronted the ways in which black Americans negotiated their positions in mainstream American society.

Du Bois relied heavily on statistical surveys, considering factors such as housing, income, education, and family structure for *The Philadelphia Negro*. This study became the first of its kind, dissecting one African American community in order to provide a thorough understanding of their experience. *The Philadelphia Negro* emerged at a crucial time. Du Bois began the study in August 1896 and ended in December 1897, the year following the Supreme Court's landmark decision in *Plessy versus Ferguson* (1896), which established the "Separate but Equal" clause, legalizing segregation. The Court permitted white exclusion of African Americans in public facilities with the minimal requirement for black people to have separate spaces such as rail cars, bathrooms, and educational institutions. The ruling confined African Americans to segregated and inadequate public spaces for the next six decades. The timing of *The Philadelphia Negro* was strategic, therefore, because it demonstrated that segregation and racism were detrimental to African American progress. By the time Du Bois traveled west, the color line in America was firmly established.[7]

Although he did not survey the region as thoroughly as he researched Philadelphia, nor was he conducting an official study, Du Bois did draw several conclusions about the status of African Americans in Los Angeles.

He witnessed what he believed to be a unique racial structu
prised not only of black and white people, but also other groups (
of color and ethnic whites, particularly new immigrants. This
Du Bois believed, complicated race relations beyond what he sa
North and South.[8]

Du Bois unfortunately overlooked several key components (
Angeleno life. What Du Bois did not realize was black Angelenc
relied on these multiracial alliances for key institution-building e
ors, particularly in business, politics, education, and religion. In fc
on elite black Angelenos, he also failed to consider the important (
butions of the working class who made up the majority of Los An
black community. Nor did he understand that black working class Angelenos and women were able to carve out modest, if not comfortable, life-
styles in Los Angeles at a time when African Americans were shut out
of jobs, political participation, home ownership, and education in other
parts of the country, particularly the South. In the years before the First
World War, local African Americans had made Los Angeles a place of
opportunity, where life was relatively better for black people than in the
South or Northeast. *Making Black Los Angeles*, therefore, considers how
African American women and the local black working class took advantage of those opportunities, which allowed them to contribute significantly to the formation of the black community in Los Angeles.

Making Black Los Angeles is a social history of racialized community
formation, cultural expression, and internal as well as external political,
social, and economic relations. It explores the experiences of early communities of color in the American West, specifically Los Angeles, from
1850 through the First World War. While considering Native, Latino/a,
and Chinese communities, central is the story of African American settlement in Los Angeles. Beginning with the history of the founding families
of Los Angeles in Mexican California, the narrative moves on to discuss
the creation and community experiences of two principal classes, the
property-holding social elite and those of meager circumstances. The
pioneering communities of color in Los Angeles were small but vibrant,
closely connected, and robust. Many faced social oppression because of
racial and class differences. This imposed marginalization affected every
aspect of their lives, leaving them squarely at the bottom of the city's
complex racial hierarchy by the early twentieth century.

Anglo Americans immediately established a racial hierarchy upon settling the region. Initially whites focused on marginalizing Mexican and

Chinese people, however, leaving the small number of black Angelenos largely alone and able to establish their own community. Many white residents in fact treated them more as allies than as a threat to their own supremacy. Los Angeles, therefore, provided relatively more freedom for middle class African Americans, if only for a brief period of time.

Making Black Los Angeles also challenges older scholarly studies (beginning with Du Bois's 1913 essay) about the black community that overemphasize this measure of greater opportunity. Most historians of this early period overstate the accomplishments of the black middle class, focusing on how conditions for black Angelenos, particularly in the area of land and property acquisition, diverged from those in other regions, where African Americans suffered racial apartheid following the demise of Reconstruction. Such a rosy narrative neglects the conditions of two very important components of Los Angeles's black community—the working class and women.

This study argues that black working class Angelenos faced many more obstacles to securing economic and social freedoms than their middle class counterparts. Nevertheless, largely through the efforts of women, the black working class in Los Angeles forged tenuous bonds of community with black elites and built close connections with immigrant laborers and other working class people of color. This interracial cooperation occurred at higher rates in Los Angeles than in any other region of the country, due largely to the energy of black-led innovations like the religious Azusa Street Revival.

This is the first book-length work on this early community. Readers may wonder why historians have focused the majority of their studies on African Americans in Los Angeles after the Great Migration. The difficulty lies in the sources available for such a racially and numerically marginalized group. Excavating the early African American community in Los Angeles posed unique challenges. Very little documentation by and about African Americans in Los Angeles exists prior to 1900, with the exception of a small group of people who managed to accumulate some wealth. Black women have been left out of this historical record. Moreover, most early histories of Los Angeles stress opportunity, respectability, and racial uplift, emphasizing middle class values and accomplishments while deemphasizing the poor and working class.

In order to identify the people in Los Angeles before 1920, I utilized several primary sources in conjunction with the United States Federal Census. These sources generated varying kinds of information, which, when put together, provided foundational information for understanding the black community like who the people were, where they lived, what their households looked like, who their neighbors were, and where they worked. These sources also yield information about a person's race or skin color.

The census takers were instructed to ascertain a person's "color," which provided useful information about race and racialization in the United States. Some Los Angeles city directories also designated racialized terms for identifying people of color. The problem that the historian must confront here is that these classifications are fluid at best, particularly when individual census takers were responsible for determining one's racial classification. While the enumerator instructions stressed the importance in doing so, it created several limitations. Often enumerators were the deciding factor in determining one's race. A light-skinned black person, for example, may have been listed as mulatto. Similarly, a person with lighter skin may have told the census taker that he or she was mulatto, as a way of denying his or her own blackness. A person's racial classifications could and did change from one decade to the next, therefore, depending on the enumerator, the instructions (which also changed), and the person being surveyed. The act of collecting information about race or color, then, contributed to the ways in which people of color were collectively racialized.[9]

Under the heading "color," the census taker was instructed to denote white, black, or mulatto in 1850 and 1860, leaving the space blank for those perceived to be white. In 1860, enumerators were instructed to differentiate full-blood black people from those with mixed blood, and label the latter as mulatto. They were also told to take care in identifying Indians who were living as citizens.[10]

In 1870 and 1880, leaving the color column blank no longer meant "white"; enumerators now had to designate some racial classification. The census also designated the term mulatto to mean something generic, "and includes quadroons, octoroons, and all persons having any perceptible trace of African blood."[11] Chinese people were included in the category identifying color in 1870, and Japanese people in 1880.

In 1890, the enumerator instructions included Chinese and Japanese as official categories. The census also became more specific in defining people of African descent. Anyone containing three-fourths black blood was classified as black, three-to-five-eighths black blood as mulatto, one-fourth black blood as quadroon, and one-eighth or any trace of black blood as octoroon.[12] Much of the 1890 census was unfortunately destroyed in a fire, and California's records were lost, so it is difficult to know how people of African descent were classified. The census abstracts do not offer breakdowns of the more precise categories. This also makes it difficult to trace families from one decade to another. From 1850 through the turn of the century, the Los Angeles African American community changed as people moved away, moved in, and died. A twenty-year gap between 1880 and 1900 could mean the loss of people who might be crucial to the overall community, particularly when that community is fewer than 2,000 people. This was an era of population boom in a Los Angeles that was becoming much more diverse.

The 1900 and 1910 censuses included Japanese as a racial classification, and the 1900 census reverted to using black as a category for all people of African descent. In 1910, the census defined mulatto as anyone having some portion of black blood. It also designated "other" as a category for all persons other than white, black, mulatto, Chinese, Indian, or Japanese. As a result, ethnically defined white people at the beginning of the twentieth century could be considered "other" based on their own place of origin. Over the next several decades, racial classifications kept changing and expanding.

It was not until 1930 that Mexican was added as a racial category. The instructions for designating someone as "Mexican" read, "Practically all Mexican laborers are of a racial mixture difficult to classify, though usually well recognized in the localities where they are found. In order to obtain separate figures for this racial group, it has been decided that all persons born in Mexico, or having parents born in Mexico, who are not definitely white, Negro, Indian, Chinese, or Japanese, should be returned as Mexican ('Mex')."[13] The census indexes for Los Angeles reveal the number of Mexican-born people, but not their specific "racial" background, except for the few people who were born in Mexico and labeled black or mulatto prior to the designation of Mexican.[14] Such classifications affect the ways in which we understand occupation and class.

The census did not recognize certain categories of labor, which had racial implications for African American workers particularly, and also for other people of color and women. The most glaring omission was domestic labor, a category of work that was held by 80 to 90 percent of black women and many black men. Before 1870, if a person was not working for wages, or was working as a domestic laborer, their labor was overlooked and unaccounted for. This meant that enslaved persons and much of black women's work was considered insignificant.[15]

The 1850 and 1860 Federal Censuses contain slave population lists for states where slavery was legal. Enslaved people in California were not recorded as such because of the state's ban on the institution. Despite this ban, slaveholders regularly brought bondsmen and women into the state. On official records, however, both free and enslaved black men and women were designated as servants. Since many of them had the same last names as their masters, sometimes it is difficult to determine whether a black or mulatto person living in a white household was a member of the family, or a slave or servant. There was a small, but significant, amount of runaway slave advertisements in California, particularly during the gold rush era when slaves were brought into the territory to work in the mines, indicating the use of black slavery.[16]

In 1870, the census began making distinctions about domestic service, claiming that it had "not proceeded so far in this country as to render it worth while to make distinction in the character of work."[17] People employed as domestics, therefore, were to be counted as "domestic servants." But the census began recognizing women's work to the extent that enumerators were to distinguish between women keeping house from women who were housekeepers. In 1890, the census expanded the category of domestic and personal service. This was the place for people who worked service industry jobs like hotel, restaurant, and saloonkeepers, as well as housekeepers, cooks, servants, barbers and hairdressers, nurses and midwives, police and watchmen, and a variety of day laborers and janitors.[18]

African Americans were overwhelmingly represented in these categories in Los Angeles through the turn of the century, with the exception of police and watchmen. Black women predominantly worked as nurses, midwives, hairdressers, cooks, and housekeepers. Designating their work merely as domestic or personal service also relegates them to particular class statuses that did not always hold up in the black Los Angeles community. This is also why one must go beyond mere abstracts in order to understand the community. Doing so reveals vital information about the families that made black Los Angeles.

At the heart of this book's research is an extensive database that I have compiled of all African American households in Los Angeles between 1850 and 1910 (over 7,200 individuals in 1910 alone) as well as equal statistical profiles on all other groups of people of color with a representative sample of whites. The demographic evidence includes names, addresses, and ages, and charts occupation, property ownership, education and literacy rates, marital status and family structure, migration patterns, racial construction, color stratification, and gender convention. In order to fill the gaps of the census, I relied on various kinds of primary sources, including material from several local and state archives, as well as many different kinds of documents such as the Spanish and Mexican land grants, wills and probate records, photographs and newspapers, maps, letters, church records, city directories, insurance policies, voter registration lists, and finally, criminal records, legal notices, and lawsuits. In these sources, one begins to hear the voices of those not represented in the histories of Los Angeles—black women, children, poor and working people.

While most historians of Los Angeles have considered some of these documents, most use only a fraction of this source base, often relying on abstracts and summaries of these materials. This database is the first of its kind on racial minorities in Los Angeles, and allows for a much deeper understanding of the complexities of their particular histories. Drawing on this data, *Making Black Los Angeles* focuses on the relationship of labor to property ownership, location of households, and families, while underscoring the role of class, gender, and culture in African American and other racialized communities. Since this database contains similar information about every group of people of color in Los Angeles, it has allowed me to make very specific comparisons and analyses about race and class.

While much of the research on black Los Angeles tends to focus on larger periods of migration than this pre–World War I era, *Making Black Los Angeles* places emphasis on the black community's founding families, who established various networks that attracted later (and larger) waves of black migrants. This work draws from a growing body of scholarship on black Los Angeles as well as western and urban history, and builds on the work of Quintard Taylor (1998), Lawrence B. de Graaf, et al (2001), Josh Sides (2004), Mark Wild (2005), Douglas Flamming (2005), Scott Kurashige (2008), R. J. Smith (2006), John Laslett (2012), and Darnell Hunt and Ana-Christina Ramon (2010). This work also lends to a larger discussion about race and gender in the American West including studies by Quintard Taylor (1994), Ann Butler (1987 and 1997), Elizabeth Jameson and Susan Armitage (1997), Mary Ann Irwin and James F. Brooks (2004), Miroslava Chavez-Garcia (2004), Quintard Taylor and

Shirley Ann Wilson Moore (2008), Albert Broussard (1994), George Sanchez (1995), Tomás Almaguer (1994), William Deverell (2005), Matt Garcia (2001), Mae Ngai (2004), Eric Avila (2004 and 2014), Stacey L. Smith (2013), and Brenda Stevenson (2013). Finally, this research contributes to the work of Jacqueline Jones (1985), Carole Marks (1989), Nell Irvin Painter (1992), Isabel Wilkerson (2010), James N. Gregory (2005), and Tera W. Hunter (1997) whose studies explore African American migration and labor.

Chapter 1, "Myths and Origins," considers the earliest period of settlement in California (1781–1848) and the peculiar role of race during that time. It also examines the ways that settlers of Afro-Latino descent affected the lives of African Americans a century later, particularly in the shaping of the California constitution as it related to the debate over slavery in the state. Most importantly, this chapter explores California as an important landscape for establishing a racial hierarchy not only under Mexican rule, but also after it became United States territory (1848), by examining the ways in which African American settlers and other racial minorities in this early period contributed to defining race on the city's frontier.

Chapter 2, "Heaven Ain't Hard to Find," focuses primarily on African Americans with some comparisons to other racialized groups. It lays the foundation for understanding the collective black experience from 1850 to 1870. It considers the racial climate and social hierarchy, particularly the ways in which black Angelenos established a community within the larger society, starting with the examination of two enslaved women who received their freedom, Biddy Mason and Hannah Embers. By examining the lives of the first families in the city, this chapter shows how people connected with one another in order to secure access to education and economic opportunity.

Chapter 3, "Establishing and Maintaining Institutions," is the story of the creation of a larger black community in Los Angeles at the turn of the twentieth century. It examines the ways in which a few settlers— many of them women—were able to take full advantage of the resources available to all. It explores how these few, along with their families, maintained foundational social and cultural institutions for later waves of African American migrants.

Chapter 4, "The Development of the Underclass," contextualizes the history of race in Los Angeles within the history of the American West (1870–1900). It explores how local white Angelenos combated notions of criminality and attempted to portray Los Angeles as atypical compared to other western American centers, hoping to pin its social ills on the small racialized communities (black, Latino/a, and Chinese) that they were actively trying to segregate and minimize. It also explores California's legal history, and examines the impact of federal, state, and local legislation on the communities of racialized minorities, particularly African American, Native American, and Chinese people. This chapter also examines the role of the local media in shaping mainstream attitudes toward local people of color.

Chapter 5, "They Were All Filled with the Holy Ghost!" emphasizes the role of African American religious institutions, focusing primarily on the early years of the Azusa Street Revival, 1906–1908, a multiracial cultural phenomenon that marked the beginning of modern Pentecostalism. It investigates the individual histories of the movement's founder, William J. Seymour and his teacher, Charles Fox Parham, the movement's multiracial constituency, and specific activities of laypeople within the movement. This chapter contextualizes Pentecostalism in Los Angeles as illustrative of the city's multicultural and multiracial characteristics.

Finally, chapter 6, "Booker T. Washington Goes West," examines the two visits by Booker T. Washington, first in 1903 and again in 1914, and investigates whether his national platform was something black Angelenos wanted for their community, given the relative gains they made during the late nineteenth century. This chapter also considers Washington's relationship with the local leadership while drawing comparisons with Du Bois's role in early black Los Angeles history. This chapter also places the black experience in the West within the context of the national experience by considering the relationship of these two African American leaders with black Angelenos.

There is some validity to Du Bois's observations. When he visited, African Americans in Los Angeles were eking out a better life compared to other areas of the country. Only six years after Du Bois published his findings about California, African Americans across the country faced one of the most brutal periods of the century. The summer of 1919, "Red Summer," was perhaps the bloodiest, most violent time for African Americans. African American men returning home from World War I faced several forms of racial violence, including lynching. Whites directed much of this violence toward African Americans in the South, while western African Americans worked to maintain their sense of community. In Los Angeles, however, whites began pushing African

Americans out of their own communities by using discriminatory practices such as restrictive covenants.

Making Black Los Angeles also contributes to our understanding of early migration patterns and considers local changes over time. The study examines the ways in which early African American settlers laid the foundation for those who migrated during the second half of the twentieth century, and addresses the historiographic gap that excludes black Los Angeles. It seeks to contextualize the experiences of African Americans in Los Angeles as well as to raise new questions about the experiences of African Americans throughout the American West. In doing so, this research challenges conventional understandings of the binary opposition traditionally extrapolated from historic experiences in the American South to the remainder of the nation, even the West.

While Los Angeles provided relatively more freedom for African Americans than other regions dominated by Jim Crow, the black middle class benefited the most. Whites systematically targeted Native Americans, Mexicans, and Chinese people, respectively, which allowed Black Angelenos to secure some social, political, and economic comfort. This, however, changed dramatically during the middle of the twentieth century when whites interpreted black migration as a threat to their community, socially and economically. Unlike the black middle class, working class African Americans maintained close connections with immigrants and other people of color with the same status. Finally, the black community included a noteworthy number of female-headed households, which indicates that black women, though not entirely equal, maintained a small but significant level of influence and agency in Los Angeles not available in other regions.

Du Bois observed Los Angeles as a city marked by people of multiple racial and cultural identities. He disregarded notions of social and economic internal conflict. Du Bois acknowledged a certain degree of class stratification amongst the black community, yet chose to focus primarily on the black elite. While this book makes note of the great attempts by black Angelenos to create a functioning, cohesive community, it also suggests notions of class conflict, which become evident even in investigating the establishment of a racial hierarchy in Los Angeles, and where African Americans fit within that context. This conflict manifested most significantly at the turn of the century during the Azusa Street Revival, a predominantly working class religious movement. Du Bois visited the city during the time of the movement, yet neglected to investigate it. The black working class responded to the influences of the middle class and elite sectors of their community by engaging in mass participation in this particular movement. The Azusa Street Revival provides a good lens for which to study the largest component of the African American community in Los Angeles, the working class.

Newspaper editor Charlotta Bass said, "The Americans who came across the plains in covered wagons, and those who followed the trail later in trains drawn by the iron horse, were interested in home ownership and a new life. Especially was this true of the Negro pioneers. They knew that it was not a case of starting again. For them it was the dawn of a new life in an atmosphere of freedom."[19] Those African Americans who migrated to Los Angeles between the 1850s and 1917 created a community for those arriving after the First World War. By establishing and maintaining their own religious, economic, social, political, and intellectual institutions, early black migrants made black Los Angeles.

1

Myths and Origins

Racial Formation in Los Angeles

California supposedly derived its name from Calafia, a character in a novel about an island of women, written by Garci Rodriguez De Montalvo in the 1490s. Set on an island completely maintained by black women, men were only permitted for the express purpose of procreation. It was women who hunted, gathered, and guarded the island. According to the story, "This island was inhabited by black women, and there were no males among them, for their way of life was similar to that of the Amazons."[1] Rodriguez depicted the leader of this society, the black Calafia, as the most powerful female of her time.[2]

Calafia, in the imagination of Garci Rodriguez, was not only of African origin, but was sexualized and eroticized. He described her followers as having "energetic bodies and courageous, ardent hearts, and they were strong."[3] The island presented a safe and euphoric space for women within the community to exist almost completely without men. Garci Rodriguez wrote, "On occasion, they kept the peace with their male opponents, and the females and males mixed with each other in complete safety, and they had carnal relations."[4] When any of them gave birth to a male child, they killed him, but they kept and raised the female children.[5]

This story is only one of the many myths about how California was named. The Calafia story represents the ways in which African Americans, especially women, were treated by mainstream society in California, and Los Angeles in particular. Unlike that mythical island, the real California was no utopia, especially not for people of African descent. In the first book about the history of African Americans in California, Delilah Beasley wrote in 1919, "The story of Los Angeles is like the gold thread in paper money to ensure that it is genuine currency."[6] Depictions like these piqued migrants' curiosity about the city. Yet, African Americans increasingly found themselves trapped on society's margins.[7]

Race relations under Spanish and Mexican rule were complex. People of African descent began their experience in Los Angeles, and in California, as a marginalized group. Men of Spanish descent defined race in order to divide themselves from everyone considered "other." This is also evidenced by the ways in which whites treated indigenous people. By the time Anglos settled in the region, a unique hierarchy of race relations already existed.[8]

Racial Hierarchy in Colonial Mexico

The first non-indigenous settlers in Los Angeles included people of diverse backgrounds. The settlers who founded Los Angeles in 1781 comprised three distinct groups: Native Mexicans, Africans, and Spaniards. 66 percent of Sinaloa, Mexico's population was of biracial heritage.[9] Twelve families, primarily from that region, responded to the Spanish colonial officials' call for settlers. This founding group consisted of forty-six people, twenty-six of whom were of African descent. Many of these people, and their descendants, rose to state and local prominence.[10]

Spanish conquests in the sixteenth century and afterward fundamentally altered race relations in the indigenous areas they conquered. The Spanish not only intermingled with those already there, they brought with them African slaves who would also put down roots in Mexico. Personal, economic, and political intermingling became cause for concern among the colonial authorities, solved by imposing a racial hierarchy. Within fifty years of conquest, the Spanish in New Spain began using race as a way of instilling economic and social control, thereby creating a racial hierarchy that placed Spanish (white) at the top, and people of African descent at the bottom. Between these levels were people of racially mixed backgrounds, whose identities were defined and redefined by the *sistema de castas*. The ruling class quickly began utilizing the system to control those of the lower classes. The system was a way to maintain clear divisions between elite and lower class, no matter how complex the racial mixing. The justification for this was to keep Spanish blood pure (*limpieza de sangre*).[11] This racial ordering had lasting implications through the colonial and postcolonial periods, especially as slaves, former slaves, and their descendants fell squarely at the bottom of the social hierarchy throughout Mexico.[12]

After the first African slaves arrived in New Spain in 1519, the institution grew very rapidly. While working in a variety of domestic and skilled labor in agriculture, mining, and other positions and while making a community of their own, Africans became a part of an intricate racial and economic hierarchy in the Spanish colony.[13] By the middle of the seventeenth century, New Spain was home to a diverse African population that was several generations in the making.

The combination of *ladinos* (acculturated Africans) and *bozales* (newly arriving Africans) contributed to the growing black community that would eventually equal that of the Spanish. The majority of black people's lives centered on the cities, which meant frequent socialization with people of other racial backgrounds. This sometimes led to intermarriage, and the creation of "mixed race" groups of people living in racially diverse communities. Yet as numerous slaves continued to be imported from Africa through the middle of the seventeenth century, more and more people of African descent chose marriage partners who were also of African descent, making community formation possible in Mexico.[14]

Since the Spanish population remained low compared to the indigenous population, the Catholic Church initially supported intermarriage. Spanish men were encouraged to marry their Indian concubines until larger numbers of Spanish women moved into the region in the middle of the sixteenth century. The offspring of these unions created a *mestizo* (Spanish and Indian) population. There was also a significant mulatto population throughout the region, and it was not uncommon for people of African descent to marry Indians (*pardo/a* or *lobo/a*). Mexico City's *traza* (segregated neighborhood) contained numerous multiracial households.[15] By the middle of the seventeenth century, some mulattos married Indian or Spanish people, which also resulted in new and more complex racial classifications. This does not mean that people were actively trying to improve their social status by changing their race. Rather, they honed a deeper sense of identity by belonging to a particular group such as *pardo/a* or *mulato/a*, which was solidified within the context of one's family. In fact, the majority of the scholarship about race in Mexico during this period indicates that most people married within their social and ethnic groups.[16]

During the seventeenth and eighteenth centuries, 87 percent of black people chose spouses of African descent. The indigenous population maintained high levels of endogamous marriage as well, such as in the Toluca region. Some people even engaged in consanguineous marriages, particularly when there was a shortage of possible partners who were not blood relatives. Between 1630 and 1640, the increase in the importation of Africans to Mexico directly increased the likelihood of endogamous marriages. When the Portuguese slave trade ended in 1639, however, endogamous marriage opportunities began to decline for Africans.

Between 1646 and 1746, 52 percent of the black population married Indians in Mexico and Veracruz. Still, the larger black population who resided in the urban areas overwhelmingly entered into endogamous marriages.[17]

Racial mixing was extremely important for social climbers, who made up a small but significant minority. Colonial governments and local elites maintained this system socially and legally. Through the concept of *purity of the blood*, Spanish men married Indian women. Since Indians were considered "weak" by way of their bloodline, it was believed Spanish blood would "wash" and overpower the weaker blood. This, in turn, served as a purification of *mestizo* blood. By placing people with black blood squarely at the bottom of the colonial racial hierarchy, however, the hierarchy did not offer African Americans any opportunity to move up the social ladder. There is no evidence that black people used miscegenation as a way to improve their social status.[18]

The presence of those who tried to leverage the *sistema de castas* to their own advantage only served to fortify Spanish ideas about whiteness and superiority.[19] Nonwhites who used exogamy to improve their status were denigrated as social climbers. "But since most *castas* opted for endogamous marriages," according to Herman L. Bennett, "the concerns expressed in the Pragmatic were white racial fantasies with little basis in social reality."[20] In other words, those who were racialized by the system were far less concerned about its implications than the elite who benefitted from maintaining it.[21] A series of *casta* paintings captured European imaginations about interracial sexual unions and the offspring they produced, but emphasized notions of racial difference in colonial Mexico.[22]

Meanwhile, the extremely wealthy *castas* took advantage of the system. While the majority of people of color struggled at the bottom, those few elite *castas* reaped the benefits of whiteness, while helping deny those of color basic freedom and rights. After the Mexican War of Independence, these few would play an important role in the racialization process in California (figure 1.1) once it became part of the United States.[23]

A racial hierarchy that mimicked that of colonial Mexico was firmly in place in California by the time the United States annexed it. Wealthy Mexican landowners were considered "white" and they used the legal system to maintain strict racial boundaries so Indians, Africans, or anyone with one-fourth Indian blood was considered non-white by 1851. *Afromestizos* and other people of African descent were subjected to the same laws that governed free black Americans in other states.

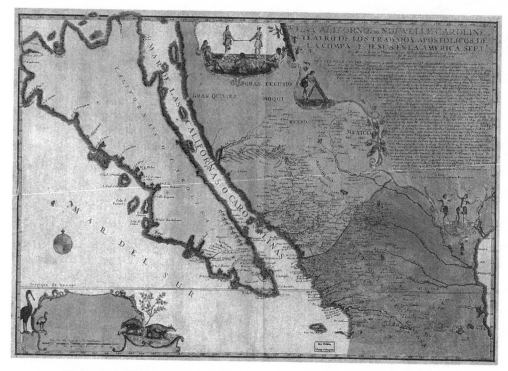

Figure 1.1 California as an island, 1660. According to a novel by Garcí Rodriguez de Mantalvo, California was an island inhabited by black women. Library of Congress.

Anthropologist Martha Menchaca notes, "These laws remained in operation into the 20th century and were often used during the 1800s to deny people of color citizenship."[24] This paved the way for white settlers from Mexico and the United States alike to benefit from the physical and racial landscape in California.

Race relations under Spanish colonial rule differed greatly in Mexico than in the British mainland colonies. In the colonies, slaveholders rarely acknowledged ethnic differences among enslaved Africans. Their principal goal was to prevent racial mixing of any kind, quickly establishing miscegenation laws to that end. Latin Americans, on the other hand, recognized many more racial categories that included interracial unions, and their offspring. As a result, new racial classifications emerged in Spanish America, of which California was initially a part.[25] By the end of the eighteenth century, as California became the home of many settlers in addition to an established indigenous population, Los Angeles developed into a diverse urban arena marked by people of various racial and ethnic backgrounds, creating a unique class and caste system.[26]

First Families in Los Angeles:
The Case of the Pico Family

The original group of settlers in Los Angeles arrived in 1781. Chosen for their multiracial heritage, the majority of the families who first moved to Los Angeles were racially "mixed," lending diversity to the city from its foundation. Most settlers came from Sinaloa, where two-thirds of the population was mulatto.[27] This group, therefore, constituted much of the racial composition of Los Angeles during its early years.[28]

The majority of the first families of Los Angeles included parents of diverse racial origins. Historian William Marvin Mason noted they had, "far more Indian and negro blood than white, though all were part Spanish."[29] It was not uncommon, therefore, for a *mestizo* to marry a *mulato*, but far fewer people mixed solely with Spanish and Indian blood. Historian and anthropologist Jack D. Forbes also made note of this fluidity, stating that "a small but significant portion of the population included people of mixed Indian-Spanish ancestry, constituting 20% of the population."[30] Racial classifications soon became much more concrete, and most people, especially those of multiracial heritage, had to make a decision about their identity, often choosing to utilize their whiteness.[31]

A decade after the original settlers arrived in Los Angeles, as the overall population grew to 141 residents, new racial identities were created. Over half of the families who initially identified themselves as *mulato* or Indian, were now designated as *coyote*, (only 75 percent Indian), or *mestizo*. They became less Indian and black or African, and more white. Indeed, some of them were now recognized as white, and received the greater social status that came along with whiteness.[32]

Much of the history of Los Angeles centers on these founding families and their ancestors, and though historians have paid attention to their racial and ethnic origins, they have tended to ignore the impact of the decisions these families made in altering their racial status. These people never fully divorced themselves from their racial and ethnic backgrounds, yet they did just enough to take full advantage of new opportunities. Subsequently, many succeeded in the civil and economic sectors of their communities. Some even became prominent figures throughout the city.[33]

The Pico family, most notably, quickly rose in stature in Los Angeles. Like many early families, the Picos consisted of a hybrid of racial and ethnic backgrounds. Santiago de la Cruz Pico, a *mestizo* from Sinaloa, married a *mulata* from Sonora, Jacinta de la Bastida. Some of their children and grandchildren were able to become white by marrying other "mixed race" people. Menchaca notes, "Thus, the Pico family was racially mixed, and their Black blood quantum differed."[34] Their "whiteness" allowed them to take on various forms of leadership roles. For example, their son, Jose María Pico, overcame many social obstacles. He served as the corporal for the San Luis Obispo Mission, managing its soldiers in 1798.[35] On 10 May 1789 he married María Estaquia Gutiérrez. They had eleven children. Between 1805 and 1818, Jose Maria was sergeant.

One of José María's brothers, José Dolores Pico, also took on an important leadership role.[36] Initially José Delores married a mulatto woman, María Gertrudis Amezquita, on 17 June 1791. Her father, Juan Antonio Amezquita, was a soldier at the Presidio in San Francisco. He also worked as *regidor*, or counselor at San Jose in 1806. After Gertrudis died, José Dolores married another woman of high social status on 5 May 1801, María Isabel Acencion Cota, an *española* from an influential family. Her mother was from Sinaloa and her father was born in Sonora. Isabel's father served in the military, was a trailblazer for Gaspar de Portolá and Father Junípero Serra, and was sergeant of *escolta* (escort) at San Buenaventura between 1782 and 1787. By 1811, Jose Dolores had become sergeant. Not only were Santiago and Jacinta's children successful, their grandchildren enjoyed many accomplishments of their own, utilizing their complex racial backgrounds to their advantage.[37]

Two of the most successful Pico grandchildren included Andrés and Pío Pico. Pío, one of eleven children, was born 5 May 1801 at the San Gabriel Mission.[38] While one sister died in infancy, two of his brothers, José Antonio and Andrés, both became high-ranking military and political officials, while his other sisters, Concepción, Tomasa, Casamira, Isidora, Estefana, Jacinta, and Feliciana, married well. Both Estefana and Jacinta Pico were married to Josef Antonio Ezquiel Carrillo, before he married one of the Sepulvéda daughters. On 24 June 1823, he married Estefana, and on 1 February 1842, he married Jacinta. Their sister, María Concepción, married Domingo Antonio Ignacio Carillo on 14 October 1810. He was Josef Antonio's brother. These marriage patterns indicate that the Picos were very much interested in safeguarding their family's wealth and influence. All of the Pico grandchildren lived amongst society's upper echelon, which was almost exclusively white.[39]

In addition to his military service, Pío had a distinguished political career. In 1826, he worked as "clerk in trial" for San Diego. He joined the Assembly in 1832, and became political chief that same year. Although this appointment was short-lived, Pío served as an elector in 1836. In 1845, he became the last governor of California under Mexican rule, and served until 1846, when the United States took control of the region. During the Mexican-American War, Pío escaped to Mexico until he acquired enough money to sustain himself once again in California. This time, he settled in Los Angeles, where he became a successful businessman.[40] Pío married Maria Ignacio Alvarado in Los Angeles on 24 February 1834. Her father was *sargento encargado* (in charge of) the Pueblo de Los Angeles in 1800, and also served as *comisionado* of Los Angeles in 1805. Eventually, he would retire as sergeant in Los Angeles.[41]

Pío Pico's return to California guaranteed him a strong social position. He opened a hotel near the Plaza, the "Pico House," hosting people from around the country, and even some international guests. An examination of the Pico House register indicates that the hotel was one of the most popular in the city. From 1870 to 1872, the register listed guests from local cities such as Los Angeles, San Bernardino, Anaheim, San Diego, and San Gabriel. In addition, several visitors came from San Francisco and Santa Clara. Out-of-state guests included people from as close as Arizona and as far as Ohio. International guests, such as Henry Sneersolm and his son, traveled from Jerusalem to the Pico House. Other guests included prominent members of Pico's family, such as Charles Sepúlveda and Francisco Pico who stayed at the hotel on 26 April 1872.[42] Since the Pico House was located at the town's Plaza, Pío Pico interacted with many of the locale's wealthiest people of various racial and ethnic backgrounds.

His brother, Andrés, also obtained a degree of success.[43] Andrés Pico served as military commander of the militia for Mexican California during the battle of San Pasqual. In 1847, he attended the signing of the Treaty of Cahuenga, which concluded the war with Mexico in that region. Andres's most prominent role was in the political arena. He joined the California state legislature during the middle of the nineteenth century.[44]

Considering the family's rising status, it is clear why the Picos, and other families like theirs, may have wanted to remove themselves from any African, and in many cases indigenous, heritage. Pío and Andrés Pico's

Table 1.1 Racial classifications: Pico family

	Jasinta de la Bastida	Santiago de la Cruz	Jose Maria Pico
Black	1/2	0	1/4
Indigenous	0	1/2	1/4
White	1/2	1/2	1/2
Racial Classification	**Mulatto**	**Mestizo**	**White**

Source: Historic Notes from Pío Pico Mansion

grandparents were multiracial, allowing them to categorize themselves, as well as interact in mainstream society, as "more white" and "less African." Since in their case a *mestizo* married a *mulata*, according to the *casta* system, a new racial classification emerged to define their offspring. The Pico children were one-quarter African, one-quarter indigenous, and one-half Spanish, signifying they were mostly white. Using the Pico family as an example, table 1.1 indicates the ways in which one moved between racial categories.

Whether the Pico children actually considered themselves white remains unclear. What is clear, however, is that they took advantage of opportunities not afforded to their black and indigenous counterparts, acquiring large amounts of property, serving in prominent military roles, and obtaining political power. This generation of Picos also intermarried, further complicating their collective racial classifications and the mainstream social hierarchy. Both of Jose Dolores Pico's marriages exemplify the ways in which a person changed their social status via marriage and denotes how the *casta* system worked within his family. If either of these unions produced offspring, their racial classification, according to the *sistema de castas*, resulted in designations seen in tables 1.2 and 1.3.

These tables illustrate the complexity of racial classifications within this society. The Pico family alone is interesting because of the unique and complicated structure that defined their racial background. Some historians note that eventually the Pico family became "white," and in doing so, they explored opportunities and advantages available only for whites. Eventually, these people, and others of similar backgrounds, identified with whites rather than blacks or other people of color.[45]

Some scholars, however, maintain that people of color did not so easily escape the category of "black." People whose racial heritage included black, Spanish, and indigenous, for example, were considered *mulato,*

Table 1.2 Racial classifications: Pico family

	Jose Delores Pico	Jose's Wife (1)	Child
Black	1/4	1/2	3/8
Indigenous	1/4	0	1/8
White	1/2	1/2	1/2
Racial Classification	**White**	**Mulatto**	**White**

Source: Historic Notes from Pío Pico Mansion

Table 1.3 Racial classifications: Pico family

	Jose Delores Pico	Jose's Wife (2)	Child
Black	1/4	0	1/8
Indigenous	1/4	0	1/8
White	1/2	1	3/4
Racial Classification	**White**	**White**	**White**

Source: Historic Notes from Pío Pico Mansion

Table 1.4 Racial classifications: Pico family

	Jose Delores Pico	Jose's Wife (1)	Child
Black	1/4	1/2	3/8
Indigenous	1/4	0	1/8
White	1/2	1/2	1/2
Racial Classification	**Mulatto**	**Mulatto**	**Mulatto**

Source: Historic Notes from Pío Pico Mansion

disallowing their native heritage. A person who was half *mulato* and half indigenous was considered *mulato*; and the child of a person who was half *mestizo* and half *mulato* was also designated as *mulato*. Understanding racial classifications in this way, therefore, obscures one's exact racial heritage.

Some scholars have relied on the *one-drop rule*, often used to determine race in the United States after emancipation. From these viewpoints, José Dolores Pico's offspring fall into a different racial classification, seen in tables 1.4 and 1.5.[46]

From both the *casta* and one-drop models, it becomes clear how one's *mestizo* or even indigenous heritage can disappear. In the first set of

Table 1.5 Racial classifications: Pico family

	Jose Delores Pico	Jose's Wife (2)	Child
Black	1/4	0	1/8
Indigenous	1/4	0	1/8
White	1/2	1	3/4
Racial Classification	**Mulatto**	**White**	**Mulatto**

Source: Historic Notes from Pío Pico Mansion

examples, the Pico descendants' racial classification became white, rather than bi- or multiracial. The second model, the one-drop rule, neglects racial heritage in another way, by proposing that they were black, regardless of the level of African or Spanish (thereby white) heritage traced through their bloodline.[47]

The third conclusion one draws from considering these models involves the local social hierarchy. Classifications of black or mulatto generally included some form of stigma. Both in the American colonies and colonial Latin America, people of African descent often found themselves at the bottom of the social order. Although people classified as mulatto maintained a higher status than people who were black, they faced similar difficulties within their respective communities. Regardless of which model one chooses to follow in tracing "race," it is important to note the positive results one may glean, particularly the fluidity of the system.[48]

These conflicting understandings underscore the complexity of race in Los Angeles as well as other cities with large populations of racially mixed people such as New Orleans.[49] Since many settlers included biracial and even multiracial heritages, the first families created a space for racial tolerance and for social mobility, at least partially, based on merit, rather than solely on phenotype. Not surprisingly, Pío Pico's own narrative neglected any discussion of race. Pico discussed instead his military accomplishments, his travels, and his relationship with his family. He also seemed to have deliberately overlooked race when discussing the many people with whom he interacted.[50]

While Pío and Andres Pico used their "whiteness" to establish economic and political status, Pío Pico was never fully apart from the African American community or other communities of color. A fire insurance map of his hotel, The Pico House, shows that its location was perpendicular to the area known as "Nigger Alley" and the Chinese block. If one were to consider the physical characteristics of the Pico family, one would quickly identify the family's African heritage. Pío Pico was of dark complexion. Judging by his skin color alone, one might conclude that he was black, overlooking both his Spanish and indigenous heritages. The Pico family served as a model of opportunity for all who came to Los Angeles as immigrants for the next several decades. It was, however, easier for someone like Pío Pico to ascend the socio-political ranks while Los Angeles was under Mexican rule, than after California became a part of the United States and American racial ideologies superseded those left over from the Spanish and Mexican periods.[51]

Both Pío and Andrés Pico, along with the wider Pico family, exemplify the accomplishments and contributions people of color made to the foundation of Los Angeles and to California as a whole. They joined other prominent figures that shared similar racial and ethnic origins and social and political accomplishments. Francisco Reyes, for example, served as mayor of Los Angeles from 1793 until 1795. Migrating from Pueblo of Zapotlán in central Mexico, Reyes was a *mulato* who married María del Carmen Domínguez, a woman of both Spanish and Indian heritage. The couple had three children.[52]

In addition to political achievements, many of the early bi- and multiracial settlers in Los Angeles acquired a significant amount of land, which contributed to their social as well as economic success. Manuel Nieto, whose parents were African and Spanish, for example, became a wealthy landowner after 1821, acquiring over 167,000 acres of land in the areas surrounding southeast and eastern Los Angeles. José Bartolomé Tapia, an *octoroon*, owned a stretch of land along the Pacific Coast in Malibu. Although this group represents a select few, they realized these accomplishments in spite of the old world racial and ethnic hierarchy.[53]

After 1821, Los Angeles underwent a significant population increase as new generations of people were both born in, and migrated to, the city. The Mexican victory over Spain heightened opportunity for black people. New political ideologies, including republicanism, contributed to the breakdown of the old mission system in California, creating opportunities for people of African descent to secure land grants and subsequent wealth, and play significant roles in the military.[54] This meant that all people, including those of African descent, adopted newer ideologies that had emerged during the Revolutionary era, and brought them west in the nineteenth century. Yet, that alone does not explain why people of African descent opted to shed their racial and ethnic heritage. Those who did shed their "blackness" retained many of their ethnic and cultural heritages.[55]

Racial Formation in Early Los Angeles

The California mission system offers another view of race relations. When California became part of the United States in 1850, the racial implications for people of color again changed. This time, they were altered to comply with American racial divisions. The largest group of people affected by settlement in California, and Los Angeles in particular, was Indians, whom the Jesuits and Franciscans sought to "civilize" and Christianize using the mission system. This system created another space for intermingling with whites, and therefore, another rung in the racial hierarchical ladder in the region.[56]

Indians lived in a precarious position in the community. Initially targeted by Franciscan and Jesuit missionaries, they were placed on mission lands, where an attempt to indoctrinate them occurred. In return, Indians performed heavy labor. Unlike enslaved African Americans, Indians could negotiate their own labor contracts with whites as well as choose with whom they worked. Indians, however, received very little protection from the *californios* who secularized the mission system; taking all of the best mission lands for themselves and leaving the Indians with very little, if any, land.[57]

Although the founding families of African descent eventually amalgamated with whites and indigenous people, they fostered certain ethnic and cultural traits, both new and old, that upheld racial divisions. The Pico family assimilated to California and Los Angeles society. They even became part of a unique group of people known as *californios*, who, on the surface, appeared progressive in their politics and ideologies.[58] Some of the grandchildren of these families, such as Pío and Andrés Pico, adopted a more progressive attitude about race, but only to the extent that it did not infringe upon their own status. This particular generation is often credited for "freeing" Native Americans from the stronghold of the missions and wanted to purge society of the "sacred" system. Thus, they created opportunity for property ownership, and in turn, a better socioeconomic status for Indians, and in the process, for themselves. A close examination of the Mexican and Spanish land grants, for example, shows that many indigenous people both purchased and sold parcels of land in the areas surrounding the San Gabriel Mission. Some Indians named in these land grants included Joaquin Emilio, a man known to the historical record only as Felipe, and Francisco Sales. Others were identified only as "Indian" or "Indians." Mexican officials gave land to their friends and families, and high-ranking officials got the best and largest allocations. Pío Pico, for example, extended land grants to his friends and family, along with white immigrants coming to the American West. He sold much of the mission land to his friends, most of whom were white.[59]

California's admission to the United States created great changes that affected Los Angeles, both in landscape and in population. The constant flow of new people into the region from other parts of the country, and from other areas around the world, influenced race relations. These groups of people included Mexican, Chinese, Japanese, African American, European, and white Americans who heard about the Gold Rush in the northern portion of the state, and came in hopes of finding gold and returning home with tremendous amounts of wealth. At this time California, and Los Angeles specifically, harbored many temporary residents, all of whom brought their own beliefs and attitudes about race relations and cultural differences to the West.

Prior to the state issuing any formal doctrine about African American slavery, community leaders raised concern about Indian slavery. On 15 September 1846, Commodore John Montgomery issued "A Proclamation to the Inhabitants of California." The document noted that people held Native Americans in service against their will. Montgomery stated, "The Indian population must not be regarded in the light of slaves. But it is deemed necessary that the Indians within the settlement shall have employment with the right of choosing their own master and employment."[60] Montgomery's proclamation was a far cry from a demand for freedom. Indians were obliged to their chosen employers and some were required to obtain written permission to terminate this relationship. All were "required to obtain service to work and were not permitted to wander about the country in idleness in a dissolute manner." Those who did so "were liable to arrest and punishment by labor on the public works at the direction of the magistrate."[61]

Two years later, lawmakers began considering black slavery.[62] The public was willing to act very conservatively, finding new ways to further explore and exploit slave labor. In addition to the earlier 1846 proclamation by Montgomery, the legislature of 1852 adopted a law permitting the enslavement of Indians. It stipulated that while Native Americans could not be treated cruelly, "Indians could be arrested as vagrants and sold to the highest bidder within twenty-four hours after arrest, and the buyer had the privilege of their labor for a period not exceeding four months."[63] Their condition was still better than that of black people. California law and lawmakers made little or no effort to protect African American slaves. The law allowed Indians to demand a trial with a jury, although it prohibited them from testifying; yet African Americans could not. Just as in other parts of the country, African Americans in California lived in constant fear of being victimized by the *Fugitive Slave Law* and being returned to, or in some cases illegally sold into, slavery.[64]

Prior to the inception of the local print media, whites used other forms of journalism to aggressively portray Indians as uncivilized. Major Horace Bell, for example, published a diatribe about the status of Indians in 1852. He asserted that the actions of the Indians in the region were unacceptable, if not disgusting. He believed that Indian emancipation from the mission system was perhaps the least beneficial event in their history. Bell claimed that since the change from free Indian labor to wage labor, Indians in some ways lost control of themselves, spending all of their wages on gambling, drinking, and other forms of "sin." These types of activity, people believed, occurred largely in the neighborhood known as Nigger Alley. Bell described the neighborhood as "crowded with a mass of drunken Indians, yelling and fighting. Men and women, boys and girls, tooth and toe nail, sometimes, and frequently with knives, but always in a manner that would strike the beholder with awe and horror."[65] Bell argued that they would have to keep Indians in order to maintain their sobriety. Once tempered, whites auctioned them for approximately one week of labor. Bell conjectured that Indians were sold out for a week, paid on Saturdays, engaged in drinking, gambling, and fighting during the weekend, and resold the following Sunday.[66]

Bell firmly believed that the status of Indians depended on whites. He expressed that white people carried the responsibility for "civilizing" them. He stated that the Indians experienced a much better condition while being Christianized by the mission system. He felt that emancipation created a space for them to engage in violent activity that they would have otherwise denied.[67] California was quickly changing from a Mexican state to an American state, especially where racial politics were concerned.

From Mexico to the American West:
Whites and Mexicans in Early Los Angeles

Race relations shifted almost immediately once California became part of the United States. In Los Angeles, this meant that black people, particularly black Americans, had to negotiate their place in this frontier community; but so did Mexicans, Indians, and other people of color, over the next several decades. Mexican rancheros fighting to keep their land often felt the impact of the mid-century violence and increased racial tension. In 1856 a Mexican man known only to the historical record as Ruiz fought with a white city deputy over a guitar. The officer murdered Ruiz, causing the Spanish-speaking members of the city to organize a protest at the city jail, demanding justice for Ruiz's violent death. The following year, someone murdered three officers as they tried to capture a Mexican fugitive outside of Los Angeles. Soon, a mob caught and hanged the alleged perpetrator. Los Angeles showed great prejudice during this early period, especially toward Mexicans and Indians. Whites considered African Americans less of a threat since there were so few of them in the community. Angelenos went even further in trying to maintain an upstanding community while degrading people of color by attacking certain cultural aspects.[68]

On 2 February 1848 the United States and Mexico signed the Treaty of Guadalupe Hidalgo, ending the Mexican-American War. The agreement gave the United States 520,000 square miles in several western territories including Texas, California, Nevada, Utah, New Mexico, Arizona, and parts of Colorado and Wyoming. In exchange, the United States paid Mexico $15 million. The Treaty promised "white" Mexican landholders citizenship rights, as opposed to those who did not own land, such as Mexican Indians. In essence, the treaty created racialized class differences while offering no racial protections. Property ownership, therefore, had racial consequences, since wealthy Mexicans essentially "became white," while non-propertied men were considered "other." Similarly, when the California state constitution was adopted, only white males were guaranteed certain rights like voting. California also limited testifying in courts and homestead rights to whites. It took little time to firmly draw strict racial and ethnic boundaries that mirrored those of other urbanized locales around the country.[69]

By the 1860s, white Angelenos sharpened their brand of racial politics by further marginalizing various groups of people of color. The city outlawed bullfighting and bear fighting, two popular Mexican sports. Baseball emerged as the popular white sport for the city. Angelenos also took a strong position on the slavery issue and the Civil War. California refused to take a firm stance on the status of slaves, leaving the subject for the courts to determine, but Angelenos chose between the Confederate and Union Armies. In 1861, the city avoided a violent standoff between local secessionists and union supporters by moving troops in from Fort Tejon to the north of the city, Fort Mojave to the east, and Fort San Diego to the south. Several Democrats dominated the city's political discussion, and gathered at places like the Bella Union hotel to denounce President Lincoln's actions. In 1863, the city ceased to support Independence Day celebrations, showing increased support for the Confederacy. This protest lasted for two consecutive years. Several army officers in Los Angeles abandoned their duties in order to support the Confederacy. One of the city's judges traveled to Richmond, Virginia to offer an army from Los Angeles. This army, however, never organized, thus Angelenos remained absent from participation in the Civil War.[70]

By the end of the Civil War, white Angelenos succeeded in further marginalizing most people of color. Yet as they continued to assert their superiority over Mexicans, the status of African Americans remained ambiguous. Although a few people of African descent made great strides, others faced tough challenges. White Angelenos feared the spread of an African American community in the city, and attempted to exclude them, along with other people of color. Whites designated specific areas for African Americans to work and to live, such as Nigger Alley. They controlled Mexican residents by constricting their activity, taking their land, and meeting them with violence and brutality. Meanwhile, many Indians succumbed to a smallpox epidemic in 1864.[71]

African Americans in Transitional Stages

Before 1850, Los Angeles existed only as a frontier, with open space for both settlement and for race relations. California initially treated race quite differently than it did under Mexican rule with a racial hierarchy, closely linked to Spanish and Mexican mores. People of bi- or multiracial heritage climbed the social ladder much faster and easier than persons of "pure" African or Indian ancestry. Those of African and Spanish descent, like the Picos, moved to the forefront of society's social status, regardless of racial background. After 1850, increased migration caused a new

Table 1.6 Race in Los Angeles, 1850

	Number
Black	12
White	3,456
Indian	62
Total Population	3,530

Source: Historical Census Browser 1850

shift in racial attitudes. The formation of Los Angeles as part of the United States ended this flexibility. Indians and Mexicans soon became victims of white racism. Meanwhile, in the context of national debates about slavery, Angelenos were forced to confront an emergent African American community.[72]

In 1850, the size of the African American community in Los Angeles was quite small. When the first census was taken in 1850, only 12 African Americans resided in Los Angeles County compared to 3,456 whites, and 62 Indians as indicated in table 1.6. Of a total state population of 92,597 people that year, only 962 of them were of African descent. The largest black communities were located in Sacramento (212), El Dorado (149), and Mariposa (195).[73] Together, these communities made up 58% of the state's total black population. In 1850, the very small black Angeleno community within the city limits consisted of eight females and four males, and an additional five people categorized as black lived outside of the township of Los Angeles in what was considered non-stated portions of the city by the census.[74]

There were only two black households listed in the census in Los Angeles, while the rest of the black residents lived in other people's homes. Only one person, a 6-year-old girl named Lucy, was listed as "mulatto."[75] The county recorded no slaves in the region, nor was there a slave schedule for the entire state. The only black head of household was a 35-year-old barber from Virginia, Peter Biggs. The other black men, William Roldan (24, from New York), William Davis (27 from Mississippi), Ignacio Fernandez (30, from Guatemala) worked as laborers. Most black individuals lived either in hotels, or in someone else's households, and came from Tennessee, Georgia, Alabama, Mississippi, and Kentucky (see table 1.7). All of the women lived in someone else's home, but it is unclear whether they were domestics, slaves, or merely boarders, as their occupations, if any, were not recorded.[76]

Table 1.7 African American places of birth by gender, 1850

Place of Birth	Women	Place of Birth	Men
Alabama	1	Mississippi	1
Arkansas	1	New York	1
California	1	Guatemala	1
Florida	1		
Georgia	1	Virginia	1
Kentucky	1		
Montana	1		
Tennessee	1		
Total	**8**	**Total**	**4**

Source: 1850 US Federal Census

Clarissa Holman (27) and Maria Ruddle (17) both lived in a hotel. Forty-five-year-old Julia Douglass was the only woman in an all male, most likely white, home. Timothy Foster (41, head of household), John F. Simmons (30), and David Douglass (30) were all from New York, while she was born in Georgia. Simmons was a farmer while Douglass was listed as a trader. Malvina Conway (20) also lived in a white household headed by a surveyor named John R. Conway (48) from Tennessee. Malvina was born in Kentucky. Becky (16) and Susan (14) also lived in a white household that was headed by a 30-year-old teamster from Alabama, Joseph Hardige. Both shared his last name. Becky was born in Arkansas, while Susan was from Alabama. Josefa U. Chosofo was one of two people listed as black who was also from California. The 18-year-old was living in Cornelio Lopez's household; Lopez was a laborer whose real estate was valued at $500.[77]

While the 1850 census only counted twelve black people in Los Angeles, there were a few others living in "non stated" portions of the county who were not included in that count. There was one black family, and one black woman from Mexico living just outside of the city. Forty-eight year old Manuel and his wife Tomasa Aguaqua (35) were born in Mexico. They had two sons, Julian (18) and Felipe (15) who, like their father, worked as laborers. Both Manuel and Tomasa were listed as black while their sons were not. Margarita Balenzuela was the only black person in her household. She was 35-years-old in 1850, and was born in California.[78]

In 1850 and 1860, the Federal Census recognized only three racial categories—"*negro*," white, and *mulatto*. Yet, several non-black people

Table 1.8 Race in Los Angeles, 1860

	Number	*Percentage*
Black	87	0.80%
White	9,221	81.30%
Indian	2,014	17.80%
Chinese	11	0.10%
Total	11,333	

Source: Historical Census Browser 1860

were counted and tallied as "colored people" at the bottom of the census indexes. Out of eleven Chinese people in Los Angeles County, four of them were living within the city's boundaries. Two of them were listed as *mulatto*, but there was an additional eighty-five people in Los Angeles County, who were counted as part of the black community, out of a total population of 11,333. Of that population, this census listed twenty-seven people as *mulattoes*—seventeen males and ten females. The census also reported 9,221 white people residing in the county, and 2,014 Native Americans (see table 1.8). Five foreign-born men of African descent from Peru, the Island of Helena, Haiti, Jamaica, and the West Indies were recorded.[79]

In 1860, first-generation, California-born people of African descent made up a third of the black Angeleno community, as table 1.9 shows. The majority of Los Angeles black migrants had been born in southern states including North and South Carolina, Maryland, Mississippi, Virginia and Arkansas, Tennessee, Georgia, and Kentucky. Others came from Midwestern states such as Ohio and Illinois.[80]

There were eighteen household heads, and all of them were male. The largest household in 1860 was that of Manuel Pepper (age 30), who had seven people in his home including his wife, Ann (25), their three daughters Caroline (4), Mary (7), and Alice (6 months), along with Ann's young brothers Charles (12) and Nathaniel Embers (11). Richard Jackson (28), John Ballard (29), William Smart (33), and Daniel Jefferson (44) all had five people living in their households. Charles Owens (21) lived with James Davis (40) who also had a large household consisting of Charles's wife Ellen (21), their son Robert (1), and Ellen's mother, Bridget "Biddy" Mason (40). There was also one other man living with the family named Houston Henderson (23). While there are no occupations listed for the women, most black men in 1860 Los

Table 1.9 African American places of birth by gender, 1860

Place of Birth	Women	Men	Total
Arkansas	2	1	3
California	15	15	30
Delaware		1	1
District of Columbia		2	2
Florida	1		1
Georgia	1		1
Haiti		1	1
Illinois		2	2
Island of Helena		1	1
Jamaica		1	1
Kentucky	1	2	3
Maryland		3	3
Mexico		1	1
Mississippi	5	3	8
New York		2	2
North Carolina		1	1
Ohio		2	2
Peru		1	1
South Carolina	1	2	3
Tennessee	2	2	4
Texas	1	1	2
Utah		1	1
Virginia		10	10
West Indies		1	1
	29	56	**85**

Source: 1860 US Federal Census

Angeles worked as barbers, cooks, and laborers. There was also one porter, one cattle dealer, one teamster, one ship caulker, one mariner, and one servant.[81]

Racial or color classifications became more inclusive in 1870, when it recognized Chinese and Indian separately. By 1910, the census considered classifications other than Chinese, Indian, black, white, or mulatto as "other" without recognizing their specific racial backgrounds.[82] One example of this includes Mexican and Mexican American, a crucial racial classification for the California Census especially during this early period, who were not separated from the white population.[83]

Table 1.10 Race in Los Angeles, 1870

	Number	*Percentage*
Black	134	1%
White	14,720	96%
Indian	219	1.5%
Chinese	236	2%
Japanese	2	0%
Total Population	15,309	

Source: Historical Census Browser 1870

The total population of Los Angeles in 1870 amounted to 15,309 people, of whom 8,849 were males and 6,460 were females. Whites equaled 14,720, or 96%. African Americans, Chinese, and Indians made up the remaining portion. The number of African Americans amounted to 134 people, or just under 1 percent. There were 236 Chinese, which was approximately 2 percent. The Native American population was almost equivalent to the Chinese population, totaling 219 people, about 1 ½ percent. (The large drop in Indians from 1860 reflects a devastating smallpox epidemic that killed many Native Americans in Southern California.) The 1870 census reported only two Japanese people. There was also a significant population of native-born people—72% of the total. 4,325 people or 28% were foreign born as shown in table 1.10.[84]

Table 1.11 exemplifies the racial make-up in 1880. Los Angeles had 33,381 residents that year, but black people made up less than 1 percent. Chinese people made up the largest group of people of color, totaling 1,170 or 4 percent, and the Native American total was 316, almost double that of African Americans. By 1890, the black community had grown to 2 ½ percent of the total population, with 1,258 people. The Chinese population grew slightly to 1,871, making up 3 percent, and there were only twenty-six Japanese people and thirty-five Indians living in Los Angeles. White people made up 94 percent of the city's population as indicated in table 1.12. Although the numbers of these communities were small, people of color in Los Angeles often lived near, and interacted with one another, which allowed for a unique opportunity that was nonexistent in other regions such as the northwest, Midwest, and southern United States.[85]

The numbers of people of color, however, do not reflect the number of Mexican and Mexican American residents. Earlier in the century,

Table 1.11 Race in Los Angeles, 1880

	Number	Percentage
Black	188	.5%
White	31,707	95%
Indian	316	1%
Chinese	1,170	3.5%
Japanese	0	0%
Total Population	33,381	

Source: Historical Census Browser 1880

Table 1.12 Race in Los Angeles, 1890

	Number	Percentage
Black	1,258	2%
White	47,205	94%
Indian	35	<1%
Chinese	1,871	4%
Japanese	26	<1%
Total Population	50,395	

Source: United States Census, 11th Census, 1890

people of Mexican descent were predominant, but the census did not consider them as a racial category until 1930. As more people settled in Los Angeles, and as the city became increasingly metropolitan, the demographics changed and evolved. The population grew to 170,298 people in 1900, but unlike earlier decades, less than 1 percent had been born in Mexico. By 1900, 3 percent of the city's residents had been born in China.[86]

In 1900, there were 1,817 African Americans living in the county. People of color made up less than 4 percent of the total population. The Los Angeles African American population was the second largest in the state, slightly higher than Sacramento, but falling well below the black population in San Francisco. Los Angeles County in the first decade of the twentieth century was overwhelmingly white—about 95 percent as indicated in tables 1.13 and 1.14.[87]

One thing that stands out in the census reports over the years is the ways in which people were classified. Early on, African Americans of biracial parentage were allowed to choose either black, white, or mulatto, which some indeed did do. Most of the time, however, the census taker

Table 1.13 Race in Los Angeles, 1900

	Number	*Percentage*
Black	1,817	2%
White	95,068	94%
Indian	144	<1%
Chinese	4,424	4%
Japanese	1	<1%
Total Population	101,454	

Source: Historical Census Browser 1900

handwritten note: 1920 L.A. County Blk population 18,738

Table 1.14 Race in Los Angeles, 1910

	Number	*Percentage*
Black	9,424	2%
White	483,478	96%
Indian		
Chinese		
Japanese		
Other	11,229	2%
Total Population	504,131	

Source: Historical Census Browser 1910

decided a person's race based on how they understood skin color. A person who was light-skinned may have been labeled mulatto even if they were not. This resulted in shifts of one's racial classification from one census year to another. Another pattern one finds is that by 1910, a large number of people from Texas were listed in the census as mulatto. There are several reasons for this given the similar racial make-up as California, including that there were many people of mixed-race heritage in Texas. Many black residents in Los Angeles by the turn of the century not only lived in a predominantly African American community, but whites considered them black, regardless of their classification of mulatto or black.[88]

The first two decades after the Civil War were increasingly difficult for African Americans, as the early promise of the Reconstruction faltered. Some black people emigrated to the West, enduring various hardships, many of which were very similar to their experiences in the South. Those who arrived in Los Angeles found that whites treated people of color poorly, and that race relations were much more complex than in the South. This, however, did not keep many African Americans from creating a close-knit society within this new territory.[89]

Historian Darlene Clark Hine defines how a community is made as "the process of creating religious, educational, health-care, philanthropic, political, and familial institutions and professional organizations."[90] Even while the black population in Los Angeles was small between 1850 and 1900, black people opened businesses, established churches, fought racial oppression and restrictions, and tended to the physical, emotional, and economic needs of other black migrants. While negotiating their own place in their city, often they engaged in state and national political issues including ending discrimination in housing, education, and employment. When African Americans first came to California from the eastern United States, they confronted the institution of slavery. After the Civil War, they turned their attention to issues such as voting rights, testimony rights, and access to education. In order to succeed, these African Americans had to show solidarity, and many did.

2

Heaven Ain't Hard to Find

The Formation of the African American Community

Hannah Embers was born in 1822 in South Carolina. As a child, she was the slave of a young girl named Rebecca Dorn. When Rebecca grew up and married Robert Smith, her father refused to allow her to keep Hannah. At the time, Hannah was married to an enslaved man named Frank, and the two remained on the South Carolina plantation raising their young family. When Rebecca's father died, she and her husband decided that they wanted to acquire Hannah and her children, whom Robert purchased for $1,210. He did not purchase her husband Frank. Robert had already owned another female slave named Biddy Mason, and her three young daughters. Robert and Rebecca had 10 slaves as they left Mississippi, racing to the west with a group of Mormons—some of whom would settle in the Salt Lake Valley, and some who would search for land to establish a Mormon colony in California. The Smiths and their slaves spent some time in Los Angeles, where the question of slavery and freedom in the Golden State would be challenged when the women sued for their freedom.[1]

At the time of Hannah and Biddy's arrival in Los Angeles, the black community was quite small. There were seven black women and girls living in the city, and most of them were likely servants who lived with white families.[2] Hannah and Biddy, along with a few other black families, not only increased the black population in Los Angeles, but they also helped to lay the foundation from which the community would exist. By relying on one another to help raise and provide for their families, the earliest African American settlers in Los Angeles created a community with its own networks, religious and educational institutions, and businesses and social organizations, as well as informal welfare agencies to reach out to new migrants who would arrive over the next few decades. As this chapter reveals, most of these institutions were organized and maintained by women.

From its beginnings in about 1850, the African American community in Los Angeles rose over the next several decades into a significant black population comprised of working class people as well as some of the wealthiest people in the West. Opportunity not only began early, but spread to the many generations of African Americans who followed.[3] As Rene A. Hewlett and Max J. Williams explained it: "The 'Trail Blazers' are those who through their untiring efforts, fought the early battles against intolerance and discrimination, and who laid the cornerstone of growth and achievement for the Negro in California."[4]

African Americans, like most people in California, promoted the state and Los Angeles as a place where dreams were realized. Biddy Mason, whose remarkable story is discussed in detail later in the chapter, helped create opportunities for African Americans. She lent money to those in need, and began a home for women who needed temporary living arrangements. She also helped orphaned children. Los Angeles, therefore, became a place where black people would settle from various parts of the world in the years to come.[5]

As large numbers of migrants continued to arrive, some residents no longer "fit" into neat racial categories. While most immigrants were considered "white," Native Americans, Mexicans, and Asians were not; nor were people of African descent labeled *mulatto, quadroon,* or even *octoroons* who could not physically pass. Some refused to abandon their ancestral identities. Those who, for one reason or another, did acknowledge their black, or "other" non-white ethnicity, faced many legal and social obstacles.[6] Through great adversity, African Americans in Los Angeles overcame several barriers.[7]

The first non-Mexican group of people of African descent came to California because of slavery in the South, either directly or indirectly. This founding group set the stage for both their community, and society as a whole. Some African Americans worked in the goldfields, while others served in the homes of their slave owners. Many slaves absconded once they arrived in California, especially if they were hired out, away from their masters. Local newspapers frequently published advertisements for runaway slaves. The admission of California into the Union as a free state, therefore, did not prevent the spread of slavery into the territory.[8]

Slavery in California

In 1849, the newly organized state government believed that the state should make its own decision in regard to supporting a slaveholding society. Some legislators even wished to divide California into separate states, making Southern California into a slaveholding state, and northern California into a free state. Those supporting slavery, however, were defeated. Article I, Section 18 of the state's constitution read, "Neither slavery, nor involuntary servitude, unless for the punishment of crimes, shall ever be tolerated in this state."[9] Nevertheless, officials adopted a laissez-faire approach to preventing the spread of slavery into the state.[10]

The early legislature profoundly shaped the state's attitude about slavery. Among them were 37 delegates including 16 from slaveholding states and 10 from free states, with an additional 11 native Californians.[11] Those native Californians, however, were from the southern portion of the state, below the 36', 30° parallel line established by the Missouri Compromise, which legalized slavery in the South. The Compromise allowed Missouri to enter the Union as a slaveholding state, and Maine as a free state. The line extended from Missouri to the Rocky Mountains, creating ways for new territories to enter the Union as either slave or free. Although most of the West remained unsettled or outside of United States borders, the territory that became California caused a schism between slaveholding and free states. The legislatures disagreed about the institution of slavery. After the Constitutional Convention for California, the ratio shifted. The new legislature consisted now of 48 members. Many of the additional members were from San Francisco and northern mining towns, while twenty-two came from the northern states, fifteen from slave states, seven were native Californians, and four were foreign born.[12]

Although Californians rejected the institution of slavery, the 1852 legislature enacted a law based on earlier fugitive slave legislation. The state agreed to uphold the 1793 and the 1850 *Fugitive Slave Laws*, which required the return of escaped slaves to their masters. This law, however, failed to recognize the status of those free African Americans victimized by slave hunters. Blacks, who were not permitted to testify in court, remained unable to defend themselves or to prove their free status. As a result, judges commonly decided cases in favor of slaveholders. Those punished for helping fugitive slaves received a five-hundred-dollar fine. Slaves whose masters brought them into the territory remained confined to their slave status and risked being arrested under the law, regardless of the length of time they spent as free people. In 1850, Congress enacted an additional federal fugitive slave law that created a commission to return escapees to masters. This law, however, was not without its limitations.[13]

Slaves who came to California quickly learned of the state's laws, and its position on slavery. Many saw themselves as free and looked for opportunities to gain this status, running away from their masters when they could. The 1852 law was designed to last only until 1853, but legislators renewed it in 1854 and 1855.[14] Slaves brought to California constantly petitioned the courts for their freedom, only to be constrained by the same legal restrictions, and later by the *Dred Scott v. Sanford* case of 1857, which further substantiated the claim that a slave taken into a free territory remained bound to his or her owner. This litigation strongly suggests that the status of black people in mid-century California was the same as elsewhere in the country.[15]

B. R. Bucklew, editor of the *Star*, joined the debate about permitting slavery in California. His statements portray a curious mixture of abolitionist sentiment and racially-based segregationism. In the *Californian* newspaper, he wrote, "We desire only a white population in California, even the Indians amongst us, as far as we have seen, are more of a nuisance than a benefit to the country, We would like to get rid of them."[16] However, Bucklew also strongly opposed slavery and felt that most of the population agreed with him. He believed that slavery should not have existed in any territory. "Negroes," he wrote, "have equal rights to life, liberty, health, and happiness with the whites, and if slavery is ever introduced here we hope the law, at least the rule, will be established to have the whites and the blacks to serve one another year about. Reciprocity could not be anything but fairness."[17]

Bucklew was against slavery existing in California, but was also against any black people (free or slave) living in the state—a position held by several others. Peter Burnett, the state's first governor, also envisioned California without black people. He addressed this at his gubernatorial inauguration on 20 December 1849, and at his state of the state address the next day. Referring to slavery as a social and political evil, he argued against the institution spreading to California. He noted that black people were excluded "from the right to suffrage, and from all offices of honor or profit under the state."[18] Yet previously he had successfully lobbied to keep black people out of Oregon, and now championed the prohibition of African Americans in California. He said, "There is, in my opinion, but one of two consistent courses to take in reference to this class of population, - either to admit them fully to the full and free enjoyment of all the privileges guaranteed by the Constitution to others, or exclude them from the state." Permitting African Americans to live in California, the governor argued, would also create other problems.[19]

Governor Burnett believed that slavery would eventually die out. He seems to have foreseen and feared a wave of black immigration. He said, "If measures are not early taken by this state, Slaves will be manumitted in the Slave States, and contracts made with them to labor as hireling for a given number of years, and they will be brought to California, in great numbers."[20] Burnett believed newly freed African Americans would inundate the state, so the state needed to act immediately. According to the governor, "They are here now,—except a few in comparison with the numbers that would be here,—and the object is to keep them out."[21] He called on state legislators to make this its top priority. The legislature also tried to pass laws restricting the influx of African Americans and *mulattoes*, but no laws were passed.[22]

Early state legislators defined their position on slavery with ambiguity but provided protection for slaveholders. By 1849, a small number of slaves in California were already providing labor. The total free black population was 962 in California in 1850. According to Section 17 of Article I of the state constitution, "No bill of attainder, ex post facto law, or law impairing the obligation of contracts, shall ever be passed."[23] The state, therefore, could not intervene with slaveholders who brought slaves legally into the territory. In addressing the 15 April 1852 law, the State Supreme Court rejected it as an ex post facto law in that, "it impairs no right, nor does it constitute the refusal to return to service a crime. It simply provides for the departure of slaves brought here before a certain period."[24]

The Court also noted that California had not entered into any contract with fugitives or slaves, even though it stipulated that the state would not permit slavery within its boundaries. The early legislature protected itself from accusations of retroactively changing laws. Using the state constitution, slaveholders, therefore, brought slaves into California under legal circumstances. The state, constitutionally, could not accuse slaveholders of any illegal behavior after the fact. The legislature also tried to pass laws restricting the influx of African Americans and *mulattoes*.[25]

Slaves who arrived in California prior to 1850 experienced varied and unpredictable circumstances. Many of them were promised freedom in the Golden State. In 1849, for example, Green Dennis, a slaveholder, settled in El Dorado and hired out his slave, George Washington Dennis to work in the El Dorado Hotel. George worked as a porter at the hotel. George also swept floors and saved enough money in three months to purchase his freedom for $1000. According to Delilah Beasley, Green Dennis was both George's master and biological father. Soon, George sent for his mother, paying Green Dennis $950 for her freedom. He rented one of the gambling tables at the hotel for her to sell hot meals. In doing so, the two accumulated quite a bit of money from gamblers who frequented the hotel. Their story was an extraordinary example of the slave experience in California, considering that they secured a decent salary.[26]

Other slaves did not fare as well. In 1849, for example, a slaveholder brought slaves from Mississippi with the promise to free them after two years. All except one, Charles Bates, ran away after learning of their freedom. His owner planned to move because he was unsuccessful at mining. When Charles finally escaped, he returned to Stockton, where he was forced back into slavery. A man to whom Charles's master owed money recognized the slave, and sold him as chattel. A group of men opposed to slavery purchased the slave and freed him. Many who escaped, however, often found themselves in the same situation they left with little hope for freedom.[27]

The State Supreme Court had an opportunity in 1852 at least to protect slave children. A Mr. Lathrop brought a young enslaved boy to California in 1849. In 1851, the boy ran away. His master found him and had him arrested in June 1852. The Court heard the case and found that "the law [on returning fugitive slaves to their masters] was constitutional." The child was returned to his owner.[28] Regardless of an African American's age or status, and although the state refused to permit slavery, the state's courts often upheld and respected the status of traveling slaveholders.

On 20 April 1853, the *Daily Alta California* published a story about a person in Los Angeles County known as Brown who wanted to arrest a slave girl under the *Fugitive Slave Law*. In 1851, his father had freed the girl, but Brown hoped to catch her without her freedom papers. At the time of her arrest, her attorney, P. W. Thomas produced them, and she went on living her life as a free person.[29] The small slave population in California increasingly managed to gain their freedom, throughout the 1850s, either by buying their freedom, running away, being manumitted, or challenging their status in court. In some cases, black people across the state raised funds to help buy them out of slavery. In others, the Executive Committee of the Colored Convention hired abolitionist attorneys to represent enslaved people seeking freedom in the courts. Most of these cases occurred in the north, where the majority of black people lived. In El Dorado, Humboldt, Butte, and even Los Angeles counties, slaves were freed, the majority of whom were brought from states throughout the South.[30]

Some California slavery cases sparked national attention. In 1857, for example, Charles Stovall traveled from Mississippi to Sacramento with his slave, Archy Lee. Stovall hired Lee out to work. In 1858, Stovall decided return to Mississippi with Lee, stopping first in San Francisco. Lee absconded but was captured and arrested as a fugitive slave. The Sacramento Police Chief refused to return Lee to his master, so Stovall petitioned a writ of habeas corpus for his property, which became the basis for a state Supreme Court case.[31]

Using the earlier 1852 Act, Lee's counsel argued for the boy's freedom based on the time he spent in California. Stovall's attorney, on the other hand, argued that Article I, Section 18 of the state's Constitution, which prevented slavery in California, did not apply to this case because Stovall legally brought Lee to the state. Stovall argued that Lee escaped from his possession while still in Mississippi, thereby violating the Federal Fugitive Slave Law. The defense argued that Stovall never planned to settle in the state, but that he considered himself a visitor. Lee's counsel, Joseph W. Winans, challenged Stovall's motives by pointing out that he never showed any signs of leaving the state, and in fact, was settling in. Soon after his arrival, for example, Stovall opened a school, and advertised for enrollment. He hired Lee out to others without setting a time limit for having the boy returned. It seemed as though Stovall planned to make California his permanent residence.[32]

For this reason, the court found in favor of the slaveholder, stating that they would not interfere with another state's laws. Judge Burnett (former governor of California) ruled, "It is the right for the judiciary, in the absence of legislation, to determine how far the policy and position of this State will justify giving a temporary effect within the limits of this State, to the laws and institutions of a sister State."[33] Since this was the first case of its kind, the Court decided not to "rigidly impose" the rule giving Lee his freedom. Lee was ordered back into the custody of Stovall.[34]

The Stovall case prompted the first statewide black activist organization to join the political arena. A group of African Americans formed the Executive Committee of the Colored Convention in order to help Lee. They combined their resources to pay for another attorney and additional court fees. The Executive Committee advertised their plans through the state's barbers, an occupation of predominantly African American men. As word spread, the Executive Committee raised enough money for the trial on 29 March 1858. They hired an abolitionist named Colonel E. H. Baker to petition a writ of habeas corpus for Lee's freedom in San Francisco. During the second trial, Charles Stovall's comments conflicted with his earlier testimony. Baker challenged Stovall's statement that Lee escaped from Mississippi. The court found Stovall's initial testimony false, determining that Lee actually escaped after his arrival in California. Judge George Pen Johnson ruled in favor of Lee and granted his freedom. In 1873, Archy Lee died. His story, an example of exceptional circumstances, motivated many slaves in California to petition for their freedom. The slavery debate in California made matters extremely difficult for both free and enslaved African Americans. It also inspired black people to create a sense of community, relying on one another through the example of Executive Committee of the Colored Convention.[35]

During the 1850s, most of California's African American population worked in the goldfields. In Northern California, African Americans began forming their own economic, political, and social centers; while in Southern California, free African Americans began staking claims to the land, primarily in the areas known today as downtown Los Angeles. Lawmakers passed the Gwin Act in 1851, which stripped Mexican and Mexican Americans of their land in the goldfields.[36] Between 1855 and 1857, African American leaders organized three state Colored Conventions, under the direction of the Executive Committee of the Colored Conventions, in both Sacramento and San Francisco. These meetings resulted in the initial Civil Rights movement in the West.[37] Their main initiatives included homestead and testimony rights for African Americans. As the Lee case shows, slavery was also a top priority, yet his was not the first major slavery case in California. But it was the case of two women, Hannah Embers and Biddy Mason, argued a year before that proved more notable.

Biddy Mason and Hannah Embers:
The First Black Female Network in Los Angeles

On 19 January 1856, the Judicial District of the State of California in the City of Los Angeles with Presiding Judge Benjamin Hayes ruled on a case involving two enslaved women. Hannah Embers, and her seven children, along with one grandson, and Biddy Mason, with her three daughters, petitioned for habeas corpus, claiming that Robert Mays Smith, a slaveholder, had illegally detained them. Smith had arrived in 1851, with the intention of settling in the state, having brought his "slave property" from Mississippi first to the Utah territory and then to California.[38]

Robert and his wife Rebecca had joined the Mormon Church in 1844 in Mississippi. When the "Mississippi Saints," as they were called, planned to go west, the couple intended to join them, but settling in Utah was not Robert's priority. In 1845, Robert had purchased a slave woman named Biddy Mason and her two daughters, Ellen and Ann. His wife Rebecca was pregnant and already had four children, so the Smiths acquired Biddy and her daughters to help out. Biddy would help Rebecca through labor and delivery, and the two small girls would work around the Smith small farm and entertain their children.[39]

In 1846, Rebecca's father died and Robert purchased 25-year-old Hannah Embers, Rebecca's childhood slave, and her three children for $1,210. Before then, Hannah's life was quite different. Having grown up on a plantation of about thirty-two slaves in Edgefield, South Carolina, Hannah had always known a community network that included family and friends that she could rely on. She also had a husband named Frank who was also enslaved on the plantation. She would have used that network of support to get through the long days of laboring in the cotton and cornfields. Being bought by the Smiths meant that Hannah would be separated from her husband—an experience all too familiar to slave women on southern plantations. It also meant losing her network of support, but her children Ann (9), Lawrence (5), and Nelson (3), were bought along with her. She would have her second daughter within the next year or so.[40]

Less is known about Biddy Mason before her life with the Smiths. She was born in Hancock County, Georgia in 1818. Her life was not unlike that of other southern slave women. When Robert purchased her in the mid-1840s, she was about twenty-seven years old. She spent her youth working on cotton farms in Georgia. She had two daughters, Ann and Harriett, but little else is known about her family life. She clearly had some kind of experience with livestock, because one of Biddy's daughters later recalled, "Their trip from Mississippi was by ox team. Biddy Mason drove the livestock across the plains into California. There were three hundred wagons in the ox team."[41] By the time the Smiths moved west, Biddy and Hannah began forming their own small network—one where the two women and their children relied on one another to survive the life they would have, as their lives were no longer predictable. They could not know what to expect on their journey, nor once they arrived.

Initially, Robert wanted to move to Texas for homesteading. But, some of the Mormons told him about California's vast land, and discovery of gold, so he decided that might be a better place to go. He intended to travel with the Mississippi group to Utah, then continue on with a smaller group to California. Unfortunately for him, Robert was delayed getting to Utah, and the group heading on to California left him behind. He had to come up with a new plan. The Smiths stayed in Utah long enough for Hannah to meet and marry Toby Embers, who belonged to a man named William Crosby. The Crosby family, along with the Smiths and three other families, made plans to move together to California to establish a Mormon colony. The couple had two children. Charles (Charley) was about a year old, and Martha was born in California around 1854. Hannah also had a son named Marion, who was two years younger than Charley. It is unclear as to who Marion's father was. On 9 June 1851, the group arrived in San Bernardino, about 60 miles east of Los Angeles.[42]

In San Bernardino, the Mormon slaveholders sought a location to establish a settlement. Because Smith was primarily interested in homesteading and cattle ranching, he set out to find his own land—a decision that impacted Hannah, since she would be separated a second time from a husband, forcing her and Toby into an abroad marriage. Toby kept Charley with him, undoubtedly to help work, leaving Hannah without one of her sons. The move also meant that the women would have a greater physical burden.[43]

The majority of the Smith's slaves were female, and because most of them were under the age of 10, Hannah, Biddy, and their older daughters had to do the work of men and women around the ranch, tending to the cattle, working the land, and doing the domestic work in the Smith household, in addition to caring for their own families. Years of physical and emotional responsibility for taking care of the children, therefore, fell squarely on the shoulders of the two women. In the fall of 1855 Robert decided it was finally time to move to Texas. Hannah, who had maintained her marriage with Toby even from a distance, was pregnant again.

Before leaving the state, Robert needed to raise some significant funds. He decided to go to Los Angeles, where he could sell his herd of cattle.[44]

Between Christmas and New Years in 1855, someone alerted the authorities that Smith was keeping several slaves. District Judge Benjamin Hayes sent sheriffs to investigate in Los Angeles and San Bernardino. Upon hearing initial evidence, Judge Hayes ordered Smith to stand trial, and took most of the slaves into protective custody at the local jail. Hannah, now heavily pregnant, had gone back to the Smith camp. She gave birth to a baby boy on New Years Day, 1856, two weeks before the trial began.[45]

As a defense, Smith claimed that the women left Mississippi with them of their own free will, and that they were treated as free in California. He acknowledged that the women had some children along the way, and that he treated them as family. He also testified that Hannah wanted to go to Texas with him. Since the state constitution prohibited African Americans from testifying in court, Judge Hayes met privately with each of the women and some of their older children. Biddy told the judge that under no circumstances did she want to go to Texas. All of her children said they wanted to stay with their mother. Likewise, all of Hannah's children told Judge Hayes that they wanted to stay with theirs. Regardless of whether they were going to Texas, they all preferred not to have their family dismantled. Ann, Hannah's daughter, told the judge that her mother would "rather die than leave her children."[46] Smith argued that the women were not slaves in California, but even if that were true, Judge Hayes knew that the women would be in Texas.[47]

On 19 January 1856, after five long days of testimony and interviews, Judge Hayes declared all of Smiths' slaves free. He ruled in the women's favor and was particularly attentive to what he considered their special needs. He declared, "All the said persons of color are entitled to their freedom and are free and cannot be held in slavery or involuntary servitude, it is therefore argued that they are entitled to their freedom and are free forever."[48] Hayes was concerned that Smith planned to take the women and all of their children to Texas, where he could legally re-enslave them. Hayes pointed out that "The said Robert Smith, from his past relation to them as his family does possess and exercise over them an undue influence in respect to the matter of their said removal insofar that they have been in duress and not in possession and exercise of their free will so as to give up binding consent to any engagement or arrangement with him."[49]

Judge Hayes also took into account the fact that the women were illiterate and had no formal education. Since they did not fully comprehend the laws governing either California or Texas, Judge Hayes felt they needed a "guardian" and decided to assist them. The judge concluded that Smith manipulated the women into believing that they would be free if they went with him to Texas; Hayes informed the women that if they decided to leave with Smith, they would, among other things, forfeit their parental rights.⁵⁰ At the time of the ruling, Hannah was thirty-four-years-old, and her children's ages ranged from two weeks to seventeen-years-old. She also had a granddaughter, Mary, the first child of Ann and her husband, Manuel Pepper. Biddy was thirty-eight, and her daughters were fifteen, eleven, and seven.⁵¹ Having just given birth, Hannah, her infant son Nathaniel, and two of her other sons were not in court to hear the ruling. Her other children and granddaughter, along with Biddy and her daughters were placed under the guardianship of Robert Owens, an African American businessman, who also found freedom in California. Judge Hayes ordered Hannah and all of her children to appear on Monday, 21 January 1856.⁵²

Judge Hayes was worried that his ruling would allow Smith to manipulate Hannah by telling her that her freedom meant that she was free to go with them to Texas. On Monday morning, neither Hannah and her children, nor the Smiths appeared in the courthouse. Judge Hayes postponed until the next day. When Hannah finally appeared, the judge questioned her, informed her of her freedom, and told her she had a choice to make—if she went to Texas with the Smiths, she would relinquish custody of her children. Hannah chose Texas. Judge Hayes thought she might have been coerced into making her decision. He sent Sheriff Alexander back to the Smith camp, hoping he would talk to Hannah alone. She told him that under no circumstances did she wish to go with the Smiths and that she wanted to stay with her children in California. Hannah explained to the sheriff, however, that she would not change her original statement to the judge and wanted him to know that she was forced to make that decision. Because she had sworn that she wanted to go with the Smiths, she felt like she could not change her answer. She returned to the Smith Ranch and prepared to leave for Texas without her children.⁵³

Despite the judge's ruling, Robert Smith wanted to keep all of his slaves, so he went to the Owens household to try luring away those who had been staying there. The sheriff was alerted, and Hayes immediately ordered all of the women and children there into protective custody. This time, he included Hannah and her three sons (Lawrence, Charles, and her newborn boy), who were at the Smiths' camp. He put them in the local jail for their own protection. Hannah was brought to the jail that Saturday night, where she was reunited with the rest of her children for the first time in almost a month. Smith and his sons were charged with attempted kidnapping and were ordered to appear in court on Monday, 28 January. On Sunday, Smith's son and a friend attempted to break some of the girls out of jail, but failed. That night, all of the Smiths pulled up stakes and fled California for Texas.[54]

After the dust settled, Hannah moved back to San Bernardino where she worked as a midwife. Her husband Toby was brutally attacked on 12 November 1858 by a drunken white man named Joseph McFreely. He died soon thereafter, and Hannah, in 1860, was raising her younger children by herself in San Bernardino. Her daughter Ann lived in Los Angeles raising her own family with her husband, Manuel. The two were neighbors of Biddy's daughter, Ellen Owens.[55]

Biddy Mason and her daughters settled in Los Angeles in the home of Robert Owens, another former slave and the man who had sheltered her during the last confrontations with the Smiths. Soon, she secured a job as a home nurse, at a salary that some estimate to be as high as $2.50 a day.[56] These wages allowed her to become the head of her own household and acquire property for her family.

Mason then began purchasing plots of land in the area known today is known as downtown Los Angeles. She quickly became familiar with local business trends, buying and selling property accordingly to maximize her profit. Biddy bought one plot for $250, for instance, and later sold it for $1,800. Her financial decisions placed her at the cutting edge of capital accumulation in Los Angeles, beating many of those who migrated during the boom years of the 1880s to the best land.[57] Soon, Biddy began using her growing fortune to help grow and sustain the black community.[58]

In 1856, after Judge Hayes's decision secured her freedom, Biddy Mason and her family formed the first social network within the Los Angeles African American community. Female-headed households, where women took most of the responsibility for raising their children and extended family members, had become the norm in many urban free African American communities in the North and South in the decades before the Civil War, and they certainly were well represented among African Americans enslaved on southern farms and plantations. Without fathers, husbands, brothers, uncles, and grandfathers in close proximity to assist, these African American women headed households that were impoverished in the North and Midwest. In Los Angeles in the 1860s and 1870s, however, single mother Biddy Mason created a very comfortable middle- and even upper-class lifestyle for herself and her family.[59]

At the time of her death on 15 January 1891, Biddy owned property located at the corners of Third and Spring Streets to Second and Broadway; Eighth and Hill Streets; and nearby blocks. She also owned land on both the east and west sides of Los Angeles. She had become one of the wealthiest landowners in the city, creating opportunity and capital not only for her family members, but for other African Americans migrating to the region.[60] Biddy Mason religiously believed helping others was a priority, beginning with her family, then those in need. She taught her family members to make sound financial investments and to use the resulting benefits to assist others.[61]

Biddy Mason laid the groundwork that led the Masons to become one of the most influential families, black or white, in early twentieth century Los Angeles. Newspaper editor Charlotta Bass noted that the Mason family was not only one of the wealthiest, but was also well respected given their philanthropic activities. By 1909, the Mason family investments were worth $300,000. Biddy Mason's daughters, Ellen and Harriet (Ann died in 1857), and her grandsons managed all of their interests. The philanthropy came to involve most members of the family, but it was Biddy Mason who set the pace by establishing and financing community institutions that provided opportunities for African Americans.[62]

The Mason-Owens Philanthropic Legacy

Biddy Mason's community activism paralleled that of Robert Owens, who served as guardian for Biddy and her family after receiving their freedom. Owens and his wife Winnie accumulated their wealth through investing in real estate and several business ventures. Robert began his financial rise by securing a government contract to sell livestock and wood to the local military. This allowed him to accumulate capital and purchase major amounts of land, just as his female counterpart, Biddy Mason. Owens purchased land downtown at 22 San Pedro Street and a livery stable that he used for business. The couple had two daughters, Sara Jane and Martha, and one son, Charles. Charles managed both this property and the business. Robert Owens became the wealthiest African American man in Los Angeles, and remained so until his death on 18 August 1865. He was 59. With the marriage of Charles Owens to Ellen

Mason, Biddy's eldest daughter in 1856, the intergenerational family connections were established.[63] Together, the couple continued the legacy of their parents, purchasing land throughout Los Angeles. This increased their personal wealth, and the level of influence and respect they could wield for their community.[64]

The Owens family properties were located at 1327 West 10th Street, 224 South Spring Street, and 742 South Hill Street.[65] Unlike later years when racially restrictive covenants in property deeds prohibited sales to African Americans, the Owens family was able to make purchases throughout the city, not just in areas of African American settlement. Charles and Ellen Owens had two sons, Henry and Robert Curry. Henry L. Owens worked as a teamster and ran the family's livery business. He married Louise Kruger on 3 December 1884 in Denver, Colorado, but passed away not long after. Eventually, Robert C. Owens would take over all of the family businesses and properties.[66]

Robert Curry Owens became even more successful at real estate. He married Anna Drugger in 1893, and the couple had two daughters, Gladys and Manila, who attended Fisk University in Tennessee. At the turn of the century the African American leaders Booker T. Washington and W. E. B. DuBois, whose views generally differed greatly, agreed that Robert C. Owens played a significant role in easing the plight of African Americans in the West. In 1905, *Colored Magazine* labeled him as the wealthiest African American west of Chicago. Du Bois spent a great deal of time with Owens when he visited Los Angeles eight years later. Du Bois went on to publish photos of the Owens business block in *The Crisis Magazine*. The family was recognized for its philanthropy and helping black migrants who arrived in Los Angeles by supporting many local and national African American institutions.[67]

This generation of the Owens family maintained the legacy of philanthropy that their grandparents began. Biddy Mason always stressed helping the less fortunate. She touched the lives of many individuals and created institutions that helped entire families and the larger African American community. When Biddy Mason died, her obituary acknowledged her as a community leader, as a woman who overcame adversity, and as a generous caregiver. She actually founded and worked in the city's first day nursery, a facility to take care of orphans and less advantaged African Americans.[68]

But there were other indications that Biddy Mason was an exemplary philanthropist and community business leader. She began several institutions for African Americans, and for whites as well. She created ways to help people temporarily, giving them an opportunity to settle in the city. She also built a boarding house on her South Spring Street property. Mason often worked with the local grocer to help people secure food and other provisions. She guaranteed to extend credit for those who could not afford their purchases. She routinely visited prisoners in the local jail, as well as patients in asylums and hospitals. Mason is particularly known for providing funds to secure the property for the first African American church in the city, First African Methodist Episcopal Church (FAME). As word spread about her charitable works, people traveled great distances to ask Biddy for help. Mason's daughters Ellen and Harriett, and eventually her grandchildren, carried on her legacy of philanthropy. All of the Mason and Owens women became active participants in the local club movement that focused on helping young women, the sick, and the poor. Ellen sent several African American girls to school. And as mentioned, both Ellen and her son Robert C. Owens hosted several local and national African American leaders who visited Los Angeles at the beginning of the twentieth century.[69]

Biddy Mason started out from below meager circumstances, and navigated her way to the top of the socio-economic ladder of the black community. Her story underscores how the first generations of elite and middle class black Angelenos helped those of lesser means, but more importantly, it exemplifies how some women in Los Angeles took advantage of the tremendous opportunity that would not have been as easily obtained at that time in other cities like Atlanta, New York, or Chicago.[70] Mason and her children were not the only ones who were freed from slavery in the famous 1856 case. Hannah Embers and her children also gained their freedom.

When Hannah was about 25 years old, she married a man more than twice her age named Toby Embers, then 56 years old, who also was formerly enslaved. The two met on the journey through Utah to California. After the trial, Hannah went back to San Bernardino where her husband Toby had purchased a small home. Two of her sons, Charles and Nathaniel, remained with their half-sister Ann in Los Angeles for a while. Hannah's modest life in San Bernardino was quite different from that of Biddy Mason's, but much more typical of other early female settlers to California, black or white.[71]

Hannah's daughter Ann married Manuel Pepper, and by 1860 the two had three daughters, 4-year-old Caroline, 7-year-old Mary, and baby Alice who was only 6 months old. Manuel worked as a laborer, while Ann cared for the girls at home. In 1860, each of their personal estates were estimated at $100, which was about $77 less than the average black household. They reported no real estate value that year, but only two people did—Peter Biggs ($650) and Charles Owens ($800). The couple continued to care for Charles and Nathaniel.

By 1870, the couple had four more children ranging in ages from 2 to 8: Nelson, Maria, Manuel, and Louis. The couple reported no personal or real estate values in 1870, which was typical because only 10 percent of the community reported any personal estate, and 8 percent reported real estate values. The average personal estate in 1870 for all African Americans in Los Angeles was $486 and the average of all African American real estate was $1,600. But these figures are skewed largely by the wealth of the Mason and Owens families.[72] On 11 July 1870, Manuel registered to vote, which was a direct result of the passage of the 15th Amendment to the Constitution of the United States.[73] The two were actively engaged in developing the African American community, along with their close friends Charles and Ellen Owens, but Manuel would soon pass away leaving Ann to care for her family alone.

Ann did not work while she was married, but by 1880, after Manuel's death, Ann was taking in laundry to supplement her household income, an occupation shared by many black women across the country. She would soon remarry, but was widowed again by the time she was thirty-five. Most of her children now grown, Ann Pepper headed her own household that included three of her sons, Manuel Jr. (17), Louis (18), and Henry (8), and two young daughters, Jane (4) and Eliza (7).[74] As Ann grew older, Manuel Jr. moved her into his home. Just like his father, Manuel Jr. remained in his job as a wage laborer, and just as his father, he owned his home free and clear. In 1900, Manuel Pepper Jr. was taking care of several extended family members, including his mother Ann, who was still contributing to the household income by taking in laundry.[75]

The Mason, Owens, and Embers families made up the first black network in Los Angeles. Even though Hannah had moved to San Bernardino, she and Biddy and their families relied on each other. Biddy and her daughters, along with Hannah's eldest, Ann, helped one another raise Hannah's young children, serving as a case study for charting black female social networks and for understanding the black female experience in Los Angeles. As mentioned above, their story also offers insight into black female property ownership and community building. While Mason represents wealth and success, Hannah Embers had the more typical lifestyle for the time. Although these families started out in enslavement, each accumulated some wealth, and even the Pepper family managed to secure the "dream" of home ownership, no matter how modest the accommodations.

Few histories of African Americans in early Los Angeles include Hannah. Part of the reason for this is that the majority of people writing about Los Angeles either ignore this early period of settlement and community formation altogether, or have decided to highlight only elite African Americans. In doing so, they tend to focus on Biddy Mason and the wealth she accumulated.

While historians celebrate Biddy's accomplishments, they tend to de-feminize her, as if she was not both a woman and a person of property. Historians have not focused on her as a mother, or even considered her connection with Hannah, or how they were part of a small but significant slave community in California. Nor have they considered the women and their families as a network that was not unlike those of slave women in the South, having grown up on Southern plantations in South Carolina, Georgia, and Mississippi. Both Biddy and Hannah were the primary caregivers of their families. While Hannah was married, she did not live with her husband—an experience similar to many southern slave women. The two women relied on one another to deliver and raise each other's children, share chores, and work in the fields and in the slave master's home, and both were subjected to the abuse of their master and their mistress. Together, their families helped nurture California's burgeoning black community.

African American Migrants

A close survey of the Los Angeles census indicates that most African Americans migrated from several states across the country, and a small number from the Caribbean, Africa, and Canada. While one would expect a particular pattern of migration, census records show more complexity. Most migrants to Los Angeles had fled the South, where most black families lived in fear of racial violence. A number of people also left the Midwest as well as the Southwest. Places of birth of parents

Table 2.1 African American places of birth, 1870

Place of Birth	South	Northeast	Midwest	Other	West	California	Total
Number	31	14	6	4	4	50	109
Percent	28%	13%	6%	4%	4%	46%	100%

Source: 1870 U.S. Federal Census

differed from their native-born children, indicating that many couples waited to have children until after their arrival. In 1870 Charles Rowan, a young barber from the District of Columbia, married Elizabeth, a slightly older woman from North Carolina. Together, they had three children: Walter, Byron, and Alice, ages two to eleven, all born in California. This pattern of two parents from different parts of the country with California-born children repeats itself well into the twentieth century. Other demographic patterns associated with migration were less predictable.[76]

According to the 1870 census (table 2.1), the majority of families migrated from southern states. Approximately 31 came from the South, primarily Virginia, Georgia, South Carolina, and Arkansas. One person, Amanda Ballard, the 37-year-old wife of John Ballard, was born in Texas. Her husband John was from Kentucky, and her children and stepchildren were all born in California. Fourteen people were born in the Northeast (New York and Pennsylvania), while six more people reported that they came from the Midwest, and four people were born in western states. Four people living in Los Angeles in 1870 had been born outside of the United States. There were fifty California-born residents, most of whom were at the time school-aged children. Black Angelenos were beginning to solidify their own significant community by having children and making the city their permanent home.[77] Table 2.2 illustrates the places of birth by gender and number of each migrant in 1870.

Early Land Acquisition

For some African Americans, Los Angeles proved to be a place of opportunity, especially in terms of homeownership. A significant portion of early African American residents secured property. While most homes were simple, home ownership was a sign of accomplishment. For some, it was their bridge to the middle class. Between 1870 and 1880, migrants

Table 2.2 African American places of birth by gender, 1870

Place of Birth	Women	Place of Birth	Men
Alabama	1	Africa	1
Arkansas	3	Arkansas	1
California	21	California	29
Georgia	3	Georgia	1
Illinois	1	Kentucky	2
Iowa	1	Maryland	1
Louisiana	1	Mexico	1
Mississippi	2	Missouri	2
Missouri	2	New York	5
New York	1	North Carolina	1
North Carolina	2	Pennsylvania	1
Pennsylvania	5	Portugal	1
South Carolina	1	Rhode Island	1
Texas	1	South Carolina	2
Utah	2	Tennessee	1
Virginia	2	Virginia	6
		Washington	1
		Washington, DC	2
		West Indies	1
Total	**49**	**Total**	**60**

in Los Angeles took advantage of ample, unsettled land and cheap homes. African Americans provided modest accommodations for their families at the very least. A close examination of African American homeowner-ship allows one to understand the extent of that opportunity.

Although the Census Bureau does not provide information on whether people actually owned their property in 1870, one does get a sense of their living accommodations. The census published actual values of individual estates, in addition to estimated personal value. The same families owned most of the wealth as in the previous decade. Biddy Mason and Winnie Owens had the highest valued real estates, each estimated at $3,000. Biddy reported, "keeps house" as her occupation, and reported no personal estate. Winnie kept a "boarding house," as her main source of income, but did not report any personal estate. Men also accumulated capital though the acquisition of property. The average value of male-headed estates equaled $1,200. Charles Owens's estate was valued at $2,000. Charles Rowan's was estimated at $400. Of the twenty-six

Table 2.3 African American men who reported both real and personal estate values, 1870

Name	Age	Occupation	Value of Estate	Personal Estate	Place of Birth
Charles Rowan	26	Barber	400	1,300	District of Columbia
Charles Owens	38	Teamster	2,000	450	Arkansas
Marshall Franklin	28	Farmer	1,500	150	Virginia
Lewis Green	42	Barber	1,000	500	North Carolina
John Ballard	40	Teamster	1,000	1,000	Kentucky
Frederick Stevenson	50	Farmer	500	100	New York

Source: 1870 U.S. Federal Census

black household heads listed in the 1870 census, eleven men and three women reported some estate value, real or personal (or both), but the majority of this small community did not have disposable income.[78]

Although family estates contained some value, few individuals had accumulated a degree of personal wealth by 1870. Sarah Jefferson, a 62-year-old single woman caring for five young children, valued her personal estate at $500. Eleven men reported some personal estate value, ranging from $100 to $1,300. Charles Rowan, a 26-year-old barber from Washington, D.C. had a personal estate valued at $1,300, while John Ballard, a 40-year-old teamster from Kentucky had a personal estate of $1,000. No women reported both real and personal estate values, compared to six men (table 2.3), whose combined estate values averaged $1,067, and personal estate values averaged $583. Together, their entire estates equaled almost $10,000.[79]

In 1870, African Americans with any amount of wealth represented a range of occupations. Both Sarah Jefferson and Biddy Mason reported "keeps house" as their primary occupations. Jefferson had no real estate value, and Biddy reported no personal wealth. Yet, her estate was valued much greater than Jefferson's, probably because she already had acquired property. Likewise, Winnie Owens, a boardinghouse keeper, also reported a significant estate value as indicated in table 2.4.

Men, not surprisingly, represented a wider range of occupational characteristics in respect to their estate values.[80] Some African Americans

Table 2.4 Estate values, 1870—female African American household heads

Name	Age	Occupation	Value of Estate	Personal Estate	Place of Birth
Sarah Jefferson	62	Keeps House		500	Alabama
Biddy Mason	57	Keeps House	3,000		Georgia
Winnie Owens	57	Keeps Boarding House	3,000		Georgia

Source: 1870 U.S. Federal Census

were able to take advantage of the opportunities afforded them in Los Angeles during this early period, especially the men. In 1870 laborer John Hall's estate was valued at $2,000, though he reported no personal estate; farmer Frederick Stevenson's estate was valued at $500. There were also four men who had no estate value, but reported personal value ranging from $200 to $500, including George Van Buren (30) from New York, Andrew Chism (30) from Kentucky, Robert Hered (38) from New York, and Samuel Jones (22) from Virginia who's personal wealth was $500. Importantly, most male household heads in 1870 reported some form of wealth, either real estate or personal. Most of these men worked as laborers, farmers, barbers, or teamsters.[81]

Household Structure

Many African Americans households resembled those of southern and southwestern homes, of both simple and complex networks. As John Blassingame, Herbert Gutman, Deborah Gray White, Brenda E. Stevenson, and others have pointed out, the slave family provided one of the most important mechanisms for a slave's survival. This notion certainly applied to former slaves arriving in the West, and in Los Angeles specifically. Black households served as the primary location for community building and networking. While under slavery, black family networks often consisted of extended family members. That tradition continued for many African American households in Los Angeles, as a close examination of household configuration between 1870 and 1910 reveals. Since many migrants came from the South, it is important to understand how the home served as a foundational and important community building block for them.[82]

Table 2.5 Total number of African American
household heads, 1870 average ages

Household Heads	Number	Average Age
Female	7	44
Male	18	38
Total	**25**	**41**

Source: 1870 U.S. Federal Census

In 1870, there were twenty-six black household heads listed in the Los Angeles census. An additional ten people lived in non-African American households. Some of them were even small families embedded in other people's households. Janie Embers, one of Hannah's daughters, and her six-month-old daughter Eliza, for example, lived with the people for whom she worked. Since it is unclear whether every non-household head lived as a family unit in other people's homes, this analysis focuses primarily on the households with identifiable heads. For this census year, the number of black household heads in Los Angeles represents 24% of the African American population. Seven were women; over twice as many were men. As table 2.5 indicates, the average age for female-headed households was 44, while the average age for male household heads was 38. In all, the average age for household heads in 1870 was 41.[83]

African American households in Los Angeles were relatively small, with 60 percent of the total comprising three or fewer members (table 2.6). The average household size was approximately three people. Twenty households contained five or fewer members, while five comprised six or more.

The largest of the female-headed households included six members. As mentioned above, Sarah Jefferson (62) had five children with her, Mary (12), David (14), Caroline (9), Julia (7), and Joseph (5). All of the children except Joseph attended school, while Sarah, unable to read or write, kept house. The largest male-headed households comprised nine members, while an additional three had between six and eight members.[84] Large households were not uniform in structure.

John and Mary Hall lived with their family as well as rented rooms to others, thereby making up a large household of nine people. He was a laborer, while she kept house for a living. John's personal estate was

Table 2.6 African American household size, 1870

Members	Female	Male	Total
1	2	4	6
2	2	3	5
3	1	3	4
4	1	3	4
5	0	1	1
6	1	0	1
7	0	1	1
8	0	1	1
9	0	2	2
10	0	0	0
Total	**7**	**18**	**25**

Source: 1870 U.S. Federal Census

valued at $2,000, placing him amongst the wealthiest African Americans. The couple had three small children, Jacob (4), John (2), and Ivia who was six months old. They rented to four adults, including two laborers, Nelson Price (33) and Edward Nibbett (21), a cook named Henry Brown (31), and Caroline Burton (30), who did not work. Conversely, John and Amanda Ballard had a large family with seven children, Dora (16), Julia (12), John (10), Willie (8), Henry (7), Freddie (3), and Alice (1), at home. John Ballard's estate and personal estate were valued at $1,000 each.[85]

In 1870, economic opportunities for African Americans proved limited. Still bearing the legacy of slavery, some former slaves continued working as domestics in the same households they worked fifteen years prior. Table 2.7 illustrates the occupational characteristics of the community. Eight out of fifty-eight adults, including two girls Cassia Franklin and Dora Ballard ages thirteen and fourteen respectively, and two men, Allen Johnson (30) and Lewis Bryan (23) were employed as house servants, usually of private families. Daniel Nichius (27) was the only person listed as "servant." Eighteen out of twenty-eight women reported "keeps house" as their primary occupations, while their husbands had more identifiable forms of employment such as barbers or farmers.[86]

Only two female household heads reported something different. One woman, C. Burton, was a hair manufacturer. Winnie Owens, widow of Robert Owens, owned a boarding house, and lived with her daughter Martha (25) while she rented rooms to four people including Charles

Table 2.7 Occupations of African American household heads, 1870

	Female	Male	Total
Teamster	0	2	2
Bootblack	0	2	2
Keeps House	4	0	4
Cook	0	1	1
Keeps Boarding House	1	0	1
At Home	1	1	2
Barber	0	5	5
Hair Manufacturer	1	0	1
Farmer	0	4	4
Laborer	0	3	3
Total Household Heads	**7**	**18**	**25**

Source: 1870 U.S. Federal Census

Oncus, a 30-year-old teamster, who's personal wealth was estimated at $500. She also rented to Sarah Smart (28) who was from Arkansas, Emily Brine (19), from Georgia, and William Lenard (9), from California. None of them were listed as working for wages in the 1870 census. Men also worked as laborers, bootblacks, and teamsters, such as George Van Buren, a 46-year-old bootblack from New York. With the exception of the two girls working as house servants, all fifty-one children under the age of eighteen were at home, and did not work.[87] By 1880, African Americans in California had made great strides in securing their children's education.

Access to Education

Initially, children attended segregated public schools. African Americans, Chinese, Native Americans, and Latinos were prohibited from participating, and the "Act to provide for a system of common schools," stipulated that children of color needed to have white sponsorship in order to attend any of these institutions. Indians of biracial heritage could enroll in public schools as long as a white guardian sponsored them. White schools denied African Americans, Asians, and full-blood Native Americans who did not have white guardianship. People of color, however, could petition to have separate schools established, if they could show enrollment of at least ten students. The board of education stipulated that the same rules and standards set for white students would apply to students of color. Oakland established the first school for African American students. Los Angeles soon followed.[88]

In 1865 and 1866, the state school board amended earlier laws to include biracial and full blood Native American children into public schools—if the trustees approved their admittance with a majority vote, and if the students lived under the care and guardianship of white families. African American and Asian students remained excluded from the public school system. The state recognized African Americans, Chinese, and Indians as one class of people, thereby excluding them without providing exceptions for one group or the other. Many prominent African Americans began pressuring the board of education, and challenged the rules in a series of court cases that eventually overturned segregation in public schools.[89]

Just as California adopted a precarious position on slavery, so was its attitude about educational opportunities for people of color. During the 1870s, African Americans in California aggressively confronted discriminatory practices in public education. Not only did education move to the forefront of African American political life, it also became the main priority of African American women who bore the responsibility of ensuring their children's education. To do so, they solicited assistance from their local churches. Black ministers helped to organize the community to fight for integrated schooling, or at the very least, equivalent facilities. Several African American families, along with the Executive Committee of the Colored Convention, challenged public segregation at the local and state levels.[90] In 1872, African Americans in California challenged the state school board to reconsider school segregation.

In *Ward v. Flood* (1874), a case that lasted for two years, and centered on a young girl named Mary Ward in San Francisco, the California Supreme Court agreed that both the 14th and 15th Amendments to the US Constitution had been violated, and that children of color deserved access to public educational institutions. John W. Dwinelle, a local white attorney who represented the Ward family, successfully showed that children of color should be admitted into public schools, and found no reason for them to attend separate schools. He wanted a *writ of mandamus*, causing the Court to force school integration, or at the very least, provide better facilities for segregated schools. Dwinelle convinced the Court to alter the law.[91]

Chief Justice Wallace ruled that children of color deserved better educational opportunities. While he clearly supported keeping separate schools intact, Wallace determined that if African American schools could not be maintained, then children of color had the right to attend predominantly white schools, making it illegal to exclude them on the grounds of race or color. Wallace ordered the *writ of mandamus*, and the other state Supreme Court judges Niles, Crocket, and McKinstry concurred with his opinion. African Americans and other groups of people of color celebrated this decision as a firm victory.[92]

The Court's ruling created a loophole, intended to maintain separate schools if possible. The justices upheld an earlier law stating that people of African descent and Native Americans could organize their own schools. The responsibility for maintaining these schools fell on these communities of color, creating a much larger financial burden than they could bear. Although local district boards incurred some of the costs, superintendents often channeled funds into predominantly white schools. In addition, white children between the ages of five and twenty could attend any public school in any district. African Americans not only challenged these laws, but also proved that separate schools were unequal, unsatisfactory, and unacceptable. The state Supreme Court agreed. With the understanding that African Americans and other children of color could attend both separate schools as well as predominantly white, black parents quickly began placing their children in public schools throughout the state by 1876.[93]

While this early case centered on a student who lived in San Francisco, the decision applied to black students throughout the entire state. Northern California, however, had a much larger concentration of African Americans than Southern California. Since the black population in Los Angeles remained relatively small, it became less likely for a group of ten or more black students to organize a separate school. The Native American population in the city was on the decline, and only a small number of Chinese adults lived in the city. It was not until the following decade that the demographics shifted, and by then, there were many qualified people to teach children of color and lead separate schools. African Americans and other students of color received less resistance to their educational pursuits than in other parts of the country.[94]

In 1870, the number of African American school-aged children in Los Angeles remained small, and, according to the Census Bureau, only 203 "colored" children attended schools. In Los Angeles, there were 24 students of color, 14 male and 10 female, enrolled in common schools, out of 2,522 students total. Of that number, 1,247 white male students attended schools in Los Angeles while 1,251 white female students

Table 2.8 Common school education in Los Angeles

		1870	1890
Black	M	14	91
	F	10	92
White	M	1,247	9,557
	F	1,251	9,328

Source: *Historical Census Data Center* (23 September 2005)

attended, a nearly even gender ratio. Two thousand, four hundred and forty-seven students were native born, leaving only 75 of foreign birth. Considering these numbers, one may draw several conclusions about African American education (table 2.8).[95]

Taking into account the educational statistics for Los Angeles in 1870, few African Americans and other people of color attended public schools. Of that number, only 24 students enrolled in common schools in 1870. The census did not indicate the amount of non-white or non-black people in these equations. It does provide, however, a sense of literacy rates in the region for this time, which is also indicative of many other factors.[96]

During the first two decades of black settlement in Los Angeles, literacy rates were much lower than in latter years, for all residents. Of the 15,309 people living in the region, over 4500 of them were identified as illiterate. Two thousand three hundred and fifty-two people, ages ten or over, could not write, while the total number of people of any age who could not write equaled 2,483. Of these numbers, only 1,286 native born people could neither read nor write compared to 1,197 foreign-born illiterate people.[97]

Over time, child literacy rates increased, reflecting the value in the emerging educational system. The number of white males ages ten to fourteen who were illiterate equaled 160, while their female counterparts totaled 135. White adults ages 21 and over exhibited much larger rates. 937 men and 824 women were illiterate. Although these numbers appear high, the majority of the white community was literate. The statistics also indicate that whites either trained their children to read and to write, or enrolled them in local common schools. African Americans also pursued literacy for their children, and for themselves.[98]

The 1870 census reported that of the 134 "colored" people in Los Angeles, ages 10 to 14, five of them (three males and two females) were illiterate. Although the census did not report any illiterate "colored" males, ages 15 to 20, it did indicate four females were. African American adults over 21 years shared similar literacy rates as whites. Twelve black men and eleven black women were illiterate. During this time, there were 373 black students attending school in California. These numbers reflect the limited access to education for African Americans compared to whites. The highest concentration of "colored" students in the state lived in Northern California.[99]

Over the next two decades, the number of families enrolling their children in common schools increased drastically, so much so that Los Angeles virtually caught up with San Francisco in terms of common school attendance. In 1890, ninety-one "colored" males and ninety-two "colored" females attended public schools in Los Angeles. Ninety-one students of color lived in Alameda. San Diego's population also grew and the city recorded seventy-eight "colored" students, of which forty-four males and thirty-four females. All four of these cities represented the largest concentrations for African Americans, and other students of color.[100]

The number of families enrolling their children in common schools increased drastically, so much so that Los Angeles virtually caught up with San Francisco in terms of common school attendance over the next two decades. By the end of the nineteenth century, the majority of African American children (69 percent) between the ages of six and seventeen were enrolled in public schools.[101] Girls made up 60 percent of those students. In 1900, Los Angeles reported only 379 illiterate African Americans ages ten and older, representing an 8 percent increase in literacy. Only a few girls ages fifteen and sixteen worked rather than attending school. Boys in the same age group tended to work as waiters, porters, newspaper boys, and teamsters, while some worked in the newspaper business or managed stores. As such, African Americans in Los Angeles demonstrated the highest literacy rate for the entire state. San Francisco ranked second, while Alameda trailed closely behind.[102]

As the new century began, African Americans sought access to formal education at all levels. By 1910, 1,115 (92 percent) black children ages six to fourteen were enrolled in public schools, accounting for almost half of all African American students in California. This increase also reflects the Los Angeles African American population boom. With a public school system firmly established, native residents of color, as well as migrants and immigrants, took advantage of the existing opportunities.[103]

Each year, the Los Angeles Board of Education published pamphlets about the status of the common school system. These brochures included annual accounts of the board's finances, in addition to rules and regulations for each school. The emphasis of such rules upheld middle class values, defining the ways in which children should carry themselves. All children in attendance were required to dress neatly and be well groomed and manicured. The same rule applied to teachers. Setting such standards for both pupils and teachers motivated those who attended public schools to strive for middle class respectability and appearance, creating class distinctions.[104]

Access to education meant an increase in black professionals, including physicians, lawyers, architects, and teachers. They formed the community's new professional elite, heading up important institutions and organizations. Access to secondary and higher education in California opened the door for African-American women to join the professional class. Several black Angelenos attended the University of Southern California (USC) and the State Normal School (later UCLA), while others went away to the University of California in Berkeley or Stanford University in Palo Alto, or to African American institutions such as Tuskegee Institute in Alabama and Fisk University in Tennessee. Many female college students became teachers, and in turn of the century Los Angeles, teaching increasingly became a female profession.

In 1870 Los Angeles, only two African-American women were listed as teachers. Grace Reed and her daughter and Mary taught music to local children. By 1910, there were seventeen African-American teachers in the city. C. W. Black, who taught music, and James Marreau at the YMCA were the only males. Six women, including two sisters, Lillian and Lania Sanderbury, taught public school, while seven more women were music teachers. Lenoila Maxwell taught a commercial course in her home, and Sarah Cole was a voice teacher.

As the nineteenth century came to a close, more educated women joined the workforce as nurses, hairdressers, dressmakers, and tailors.[105] It is in this context that African Americans in Los Angeles, especially women, created and maintained institutions that allowed them to extend beyond their familial walls, out into the black community as a whole. They opened their homes, secured property, founded religious establishments, fought for educational opportunities, and created employment opportunities. This made it easier for new migrants who came to the city at the beginning of the twentieth century to settle into a well-established black community in the West.

3

Establishing and Maintaining Institutions

On 10 September 1910, a woman named Charlotta traveled from Providence, Rhode Island to Los Angeles where she planned to recuperate from an illness. She expected to soak up the warm weather and sunshine for a maximum of two years—her stay ended up lasting almost sixty years. In fact, Charlotta Bass made Los Angeles her permanent home and final resting place on 12 April 1969, when she was buried at the Evergreen Cemetery. For almost sixty years, Bass fought for African American rights in Los Angeles and Southern California.[1]

Bass recalled that she chose Los Angeles because her doctor advised her that an extended stay in the warmth of the California sunshine would improve her ailing health. Even in 1910, the cost of living in Los Angeles was extremely high, so Bass sought employment to ease the incurring expenses. She collected subscriptions for the *California Eagle*, which, at that time, was among the small handful of African American-owned newspapers in Los Angeles. Until then, Bass's only experience with newspaper publications occurred in Providence, where she worked as an office girl and subscription solicitor.[2]

Not long after Bass began working at the *Eagle*, her employer, John J. Neimore complained that his readers overlooked him and wished more people accepted his ideology. He expected people to support his efforts in creating and maintaining the city's leading and most progressive African American newspaper. Neimore, a 35-year-old from Texas, along with his 26-year-old wife, Ida B. from Tennessee, had founded *The California Eagle* in 1879 and ran it until 1912 when he relinquished the newspaper to Bass. Bass noted that the *Eagle* was Neimore's life, and his dedication was unmatched. When Neimore became ill, Bass readily stepped in to help.[3]

Bass initially worked for the *Eagle* at a salary of $5.00 per week, but after Neimore's death, became the *Eagle*'s editor, a position she held for the next forty years. She and her husband, Joseph, dedicated their lives to the *Eagle*. Their newspaper was committed to the struggle for civil rights and racial equality. They also highlighted the socially elite side of

African American life in Los Angeles that mainstream newspapers such as the *Los Angeles Times* and the *Herald* so grossly overlooked.[4]

In addition to being the premier African American newspaper in Los Angeles and Southern California, the *California Eagle* initially sought to represent all marginalized groups of people of color. The paper staffed a diverse group of employees, representing three of the largest groups of people living in the city. African Americans worked alongside both whites and Mexican Americans, and as Bass pointed out, they got along quite well. At the beginning of the twentieth century, African American printers migrated to the city in search of jobs, but faced discrimination. A move to exclude African Americans from the newspaper business began, and the *California Eagle* became a place of solace for some of them. The *Eagle* remained the leading source of information for African Americans throughout most of the twentieth century until it closed down in 1965.[5]

Only three years after Bass's arrival in Los Angeles, in 1913, W. E. B. Du Bois visited California. After touring the city and surrounding locales, he compared the status of black Angelenos to middle class African Americans throughout the country, noting their many accomplishments. Understanding the notion of the "California Dream" as a paradise, and Los Angeles as a picture perfect place for prosperity, Du Bois promoted the state and the city in the *Crisis Magazine*. He determined that Los Angeles offered the best opportunity for urban-bound African Americans. Du Bois also presented black Angelenos as successful and prosperous. While noting some working-class issues, Du Bois focused primarily on the black elite. Migrants dealt with not only a separate culture of people, but also a smaller African American community, which made establishing themselves slightly easier.[6]

This chapter explores the experiences of the African American community in Los Angeles between 1870 and the 1920s, just after African Americans and other people of color again found themselves segregated throughout the city. It considers social and religious institutions as well as others, created and maintained by local African Americans. It also examines the ways in which many black people used these institutions as a means to bolster the community more broadly.[7]

The African American community in Los Angeles at the turn of the century can be defined in part by its social, economic, and religious networks, many of which fell into the tradition of black self-help organizations prominent on the East Coast and in the South since the 18th century. Many black Angelenos organized and maintained such self-help programs, and numerous social and religious institutions, and fought for the educational rights of African Americans and other people of color. The community itself consisted of elite, middle, and working class black Angelenos, who often relied on one another to combat racism.

Many African Americans did not have similar means as whites, but were able to afford houses and even undeveloped land for themselves and their families. Being able to buy even modest accommodations helped African Americans accumulate more wealth than others who either rented rooms or homes. Collectively, the black community provided the foundation for the black middle class, who took on the responsibility for advancing the race, and whose efforts engendered philanthropic ventures that affected the entire community. Members of the middle class reached out to those less fortunate, creating unique opportunities for newcomers.[8]

Patterns of Migration

California's early years reflected a small but significant amount of African American migration into the region, numbers that increased sharply around the turn of the century. In the years immediately following the Civil War, a number of black families in Los Angeles laid the ground-work for establishing a solid community. Between 1870 and 1880, black migration patterns reflected those of previous years. Thirty-five people came from the South, such as Virginia, Maryland, and Georgia. Ten more people came from other countries such as Bermuda, Jamaica, the Philippines, France and Ireland. One person listed Africa as their place of birth. Two people from Ireland were listed as "mulatto," but only one of them, Marcelina Fyleaku was married to an African American. The others were married to white partners. Of the two Jamaicans listed, one, Horatio Marteen, was labeled "mulatto."[9] Table 3.1 shows the numbers of black people in Los Angeles who were born in California as well as other states by 1880.

African Americans from Texas had not migrated to the region by 1880, nor were there any black people who listed Mexico as their place of birth. Many came from northeastern states like New York and Pennsylvania. Only one person, 10-year-old Charles Cook, reported being born in the West but outside California (Cook came from Nevada). His other four siblings were born in Maryland and Pennsylvania like their parents. Eleven people reported the Midwest as their birthplace, coming from

Table 3.1 African American places of birth by gender, 1880

Place of Birth	Female	Place of Birth	Male
Arkansas	1	Africa	1
California	18	Arkansas	1
District of Columbia	1	Bermuda	1
Georgia	4	California	20
Indiana	1	Connecticut	1
Ireland	2	France	1
Jamaica	1	Ireland	2
Maryland	3	Jamaica	1
Mississippi	5	Kentucky	1
Missouri	5	Louisiana	3
New York	1	Manila	1
Pennsylvania	2	Maryland	3
South Carolina	1	Mississippi	1
Virginia	2	Missouri	4
		Nevada	1
		New York	4
		North Carolina	1
		Ohio	1
		Pennsylvania	3
		Rhode Island	1
		South Carolina	1
		Virginia	2
		Unknown	1
Total	**47**	**Total**	**56**

Source: 1870 U.S. Federal Census

Ohio, Missouri, and Kansas. The number of immigrants of African descent had doubled since the previous decade with places of origin also including Africa, Jamaica, and the West Indies.[10] Table 3.2 summarizes this regional data.

At the turn of the century, not only did the African American population increase significantly, migrants came from all regions of the country. While parents migrated from different states, most children were born in California, solidifying a generation of native-born African Americans. Stephen Miller, born in South Carolina, for example, married Elizabeth, who was from Texas, but both of their children, Robert and Rebecca, ages eight and four respectively, were California-born.

Table 3.2 African American places of birth, 1880

Place of Birth	South	Southwest	Northeast	Midwest	Other Countries	West	Unknown	California
Number	30	0	12	11	11	1	1	38
Percent	30%	0%	12%	11%	10%	<1%	<1%	37%

Source: 1880 U.S. Federal Census

Seven hundred and ten people migrated from the southern states. People from the Southwest equaled 20 percent of the entire African American population in Los Angeles. More people from the Northeast and Midwest also migrated to Los Angeles: 262 Midwesterners from Kansas, Missouri, and Ohio. Those from the Northeast came from New York, Pennsylvania, New Jersey, and Rhode Island. A small population of foreign-born black people also came to Los Angeles, while forty-two people reported unknown places of birth. Six people reported Western states as their place of birth. Finally, the 1900 census listed three people from Indian Territory. These reported numbers are reflected in table 3.3. The regional background of the African American population of 1900 transformed significantly from its 1880 figures, as indicated in table 3.4.[11]

By 1910, more African Americans came the city from various states and other parts of the world. Southern migrants made up almost half of the African American migration into Los Angeles by that year, as table 3.5 illustrates.[12] While the largest increase in migrants were born in Texas (1,269), people born in Georgia (1,044) and California-born residents (1,052) made up the second largest groups of Los Angeles's black residents by 1910. Other states representing large numbers of migrants that decade (tables 3.6a and 3.6b) included Missouri (461), Tennessee (376), Louisiana (404), and Alabama (326).

As the years went on, parents increasingly reported having different places of birth than their children. By 1910 most black children in Los Angeles were born in California.[13] This increasingly settled lifestyle meant that African Americans were able to maintain a significant and functioning community that would surpass that of other western American cities such as Denver, San Francisco, Oakland, Omaha, and Seattle.[14] In order to do so, they began establishing crucial social institutions, led primarily by black Angeleno women, who made up just over half of the entire black population (51 percent).

Table 3.3 African American places of birth by gender, 1900

Place of Birth	Women	Place of Birth	Men
Alabama	46	Alabama	42
Arkansas	59	Arizona	1
California	222	Arkansas	10
Canada	5	California	201
Colorado	2	Canada	4
Georgia	78	Colorado	2
Illinois	13	Cuba	1
Indian Territory	2	England	1
Indiana	1	Florida	1
Iowa	14	Georgia	76
Ireland	5	Illinois	14
Jamaica	1	Indian Territory	1
Kansas	25	Indiana	2
Kentucky	29	Iowa	8
Louisiana	37	Ireland	1
Maryland	6	Jamaica	2
Massachusetts	1	Kansas	18
Mexico	1	Kentucky	41
Michigan	7	Louisiana	25
Minnesota	1	Maryland	5
Mississippi	31	Massachusetts	2
Missouri	66	Michigan	5
Nebraska	2	Minnesota	2
Nevada	1	Mississippi	14
New Jersey	1	Missouri	51
New Mexico	2	Nevada	1
New York	8	New Jersey	1
North Carolina	25	New Mexico	2
Ohio	9	New York	16
Pennsylvania	7	North Carolina	20
South Carolina	15	Ohio	23
Tennessee	61	Oklahoma	1
Texas	200	Pennsylvania	11
Utah	3	Rhode Island	1
Virginia	26	South Carolina	15
Washington	1	Tennessee	52
Washington, DC	2	Texas	173
West Virginia	2	Trinidad	1
Wisconsin	1	Utah	3

Table 3.3 (continued)

Place of Birth	Women	Place of Birth	Men
Unknown	17	Virginia	38
		Washington	2
		West Indies	4
		Washington, DC	7
		West Virginia	4
		Wisconsin	1
		Unknown	25
Total	**991**	**Total**	**931**

Source: 1900 U.S. Federal Census

Table 3.4 African American places of birth, 1900

Place of Birth	South	Southwest	Northeast	Midwest	Other	West	Unknown	California
Number	710	380	47	262	30	5	60	392
Percent	38%	20%	2%	14%	1.5%	<1%	3%	21%

Source: 1900 U.S. Federal Census

Table 3.5 African American places of birth, 1910

Place of Birth	South	Southwest	Northeast	Midwest	Other	West	Unknown	California	
Number	3391	1370	198	990	157	76	25	1005	7212
Percent	47%	19%	3%	14%	2%	1%	<1%	14%	100%

Source: 1910 U.S. Federal Census

Social Networks and Institution Building

Between 1850 and 1900, many female black Angelenos opened their homes to newly arriving migrants, establishing private networks that helped people secure food, housing, and employment, and to make social connections. Building on the tradition of mutual aid established by Biddy Mason and Winnie Owens in the 1870s, several African American women owned and operated small boardinghouses, or simply provided temporary lodging for others. Of the 105 female household heads in Los Angeles in

Table 3.6a African American places of birth for women, 1910

Place of Birth	Women	Place of Birth	Women
Alabama	156	Massachusetts	11
Arizona	9	Mexico	6
Arkansas	112	Michigan	16
At sea (Bermuda)	3	Minnesota	4
Bohemia	1	Mississippi	94
California	543	Missouri	252
Canada	18	Montana	1
Colorado	19	Nebraska	2
Connecticut	6	New Jersey	5
Cuba	1	New Mexico	11
Dakota	1	New York	13
Delaware	1	North Carolina	63
England	1	Ohio	58
Florida	28	Oklahoma	37
Georgia	527	Oregon	2
Germany	2	Pennsylvania	14
Grenada	2	Poland	1
Guatemala	1	Rhode Island	2
Hungary	1	South Carolina	87
Idaho	1	Tennessee	196
Illinois	47	Texas	683
India	1	United States	20
Indian Territory	7	Unknown	7
Indiana	19	Utah	6
Iowa	17	Vermont	2
Jamaica	2	Virginia	97
Kansas	104	Washington	6
Kentucky	132	Washington, DC	17
Louisiana	222	West Indies	1
Maine	2	West Virginia	3
Maryland	15	Wisconsin	1
Total			**3719**

Source: 1910 U.S. Federal Census

Table 3.6b African American places of birth for men, 1910

Place of Birth	Men	Place of Birth	Men
Africa	3	Maryland	17
Alabama	170	Massachusetts	13
Arizona	8	Mexico	5
Arkansas	102	Michigan	12
Australia	2	Minnesota	1
California	462	Mississippi	101
Canada	15	Missouri	209
China	2	Montana	4
Colorado	14	Nebraska	2
Connecticut	5	Nevada	2
Cuba	3	New Jersey	6
Delaware	2	New Mexico	10
Denmark	1	New York	18
England	3	North Carolina	60
Florida	41	Ohio	58
France	2	Oklahoma	26
Georgia	520	Oregon	2
Germany	0	Pennsylvania	30
Greek Territory	1	Philippines	1
Grenada	2	Puerto Rico	1
Guatemala	1	South Carolina	81
Haiti	1	St Kitts	1
Hawaii	2	Tennessee	180
Illinois	53	Texas	586
Indian Territory	4	United States	38
Indiana	21	Unknown	18
Iowa	18	Utah	2
Ireland	1	Virginia	89
Jamaica	3	Washington	3
Japan	2	Washington, DC	16
Kansas	94	West Indies	8
Kentucky	144	West Virginia	4
Louisiana	182	Wisconsin	1
Maine	3	Wyoming	1
Total			**3493**

Source: 1910 U.S. Federal Census

1900, 24 percent shared their homes. Two women, Ida Young and Mary Harris, listed boardinghouse keeper as their occupation, while six identified themselves as keepers of lodging houses. Annie Melhado was the only woman who identified herself as keeper of a lodging house who was not the head of her own household. At the time of the 1900 census, there were no lodgers residing in the home she and her husband Charles rented on Vine Street.[15]

The majority of boardinghouses run by black women in Los Angeles were homes with less than two lodgers or boarders, and they contained several configurations. Ten households had male renters, compared to five with women. Four homes contained both male and female renters, while three took in children. Mary Witts, for example, rented rooms to one couple, Joseph and Mattie Lafayette, but also took in six children, three boys and three girls, less than five years of age, perhaps providing foster care. At least half of all black women who provided lodging in Los Angeles were widowed. Some also provided jobs such as laundry and ironing for renters. Many female household heads in early twentieth-century Los Angeles, therefore, served as temporary employment and housing outlets for newly arriving migrants, as some boarders worked with the women washing and ironing, while others helped by paying a portion of the rent or mortgage.[16]

Many black Californian women engaged in several charitable activities, mostly in spaces provided by the African American church, or else in their own homes. Most of these activities could be found in cities with the largest concentrations of black residents. The first recorded "uplift" group began in 1859 in Placerville (northern California). In 1860, black San Franciscan women organized the Ladies' Benevolent Society and the Ladies' Pacific Accommodating and Benevolent Society. The following year, women in Sacramento (the state's largest black population) organized the first women's auxiliary to a chapter of a men's fraternal organization, the Eastern Star. Los Angeles also had a very active club movement. Through these organizations, women raised money by holding "ladies' festivals," teas, picnics, and food fairs.[17]

Much of the charitable work sponsored by African American women's church groups was designed to help young children obtain an education. Women from the Wesley Chapel AME Church, for example, organized the Women's Day Nursery Association in 1907, which helped children attending the public schools. The women created a nursery for younger children and provided lunch and sometimes dinner for African American public school children. Women at the First African Methodist Episcopal church organized the Negro Nursery Association and the Child Study Circle in May 1908. In addition to helping school children, African American clubwomen in Los Angeles organized programs around their own cultural and intellectual heritage including dramatic readings, plays, and musicals written by African Americans.[18]

Black Angelenos first formed their community ties by establishing religious institutions. The Owens household (see chapter 2) was initially the gathering place for business and religious meetings. In 1872, Biddy Mason paid the taxes and other expenses for the First African Methodist Episcopal (FAME) church to organize as an independent entity. FAME was an African American congregation, independent of other churches with predominantly white memberships. This created a separate organization for African Americans to control their own institution and spiritual doctrine. Mason even helped FAME to purchase its first church building, located on the east side of downtown, on Los Angeles and Azusa Streets.[19]

By 1885, Los Angeles had a second African American church as well, Second Baptist. Together, these churches served the majority of the African American community, spiritually as well as socially. Both acted as the major religious institutions for the remainder of the nineteenth century. As other black churches organized across the city, these two were where most African Americans in the city attended worship services.[20]

According to Charlotta Bass, both First AME and Second Baptist churches served as the "mega" churches of the early periods. They provided educational facilities, gave assistance to working class people, held social and political meetings, and kept the African American population united. By the turn of the twentieth century, Los Angeles had several African American churches, each designed for meeting the particular needs of its congregation. The Wesley Chapel was founded in 1888, followed by Mount Zion Missionary Baptist Church (1892), then Tabernacle Baptist and New Hope Baptist churches in 1897. While new branches of older churches were organizing, such as the African Methodist Episcopal Zion (AMEZ) church (1906), other churches also organized, like the Westminster Presbyterian Church (1904) and the Pentecostal, Apostolic Faith Mission in 1906.[21]

The black church in Los Angeles was the first institution operated by local African Americans that allowed them complete autonomy. These churches often served as conduits for African Americans to obtain education and social welfare, as well as spiritual guidance. They served as the center of African American life. When most African Americans arrived in Los Angeles, they found themselves drawn to one of the city's black churches to gain a sense of community and reestablish cultural ties.[22] The women in these churches organized their own clubs and auxiliaries to address the needs of the black community in general, but specifically to deal directly with women's issues.[23]

The black churches gave women a platform—and a space—to organize social welfare activities and to participate in social reform campaigns, that served a variety of needs. Religious institutions also provided them a venue to address many of the community's needs such as providing medical aid and burial services. The clubs hosted evenings of literature to support local political organizations, as did women's groups in Boston, Philadelphia, Grand Rapids, Chicago, Detroit, Denver, Atlanta, New Orleans, Washington, D.C., and New York. Indeed, most African American women's charity and fundraising work was organized through the church in the nineteenth and early twentieth centuries.[24]

Evelyn Brooks Higginbotham explains that the church "housed a diversity of programs including schools, circulating libraries, concerts, restaurants, insurance companies, vocational training, athletic clubs—all catering to a population much broader than the membership of individual churches."[25] This gave women a platform to organize several "uplift" agencies focused on reform efforts, ranging from temperance to salvation. Higginbotham notes that the church offered women "a forum through which to articulate a public discourse critical to women's subordination."[26] Through these outlets, black women in Los Angeles were able to address many of the community's needs, including "racism, sexism, and poverty,"[27] according to Bettye Collier-Thomas. Most of their charity and fundraising work occurred in the very churches they established.

By the early 1900s, the African American club movement was well underway in Los Angeles. Black middle-class women focused their efforts on racial uplift. Securing housing and employment, and helping the sick and the poor, were their primary objectives. Many women, for example, joined the Sojourner Truth Industrial Club. Founded in 1904, and modeled after the Philadelphia and Chicago branches, the Los Angeles chapter of this club maintained the objective of making a successful, "self-sustaining home for women."[28]

The Women's Progressive Club was organized in 1903, and focused on literary activities. Its members read and met to discuss the works of

William Shakespeare and other famous writers. In 1909 the group elected to apply for an affiliation with the National Federation. The Young Women's Dramatic Club, founded in 1904, raised literary awareness by performing "thought inspiring" dramatic pieces of literature. Proceeds from their performances were used to help children attend school and to promote literacy among the community.[29]

Kate Bradley-Stovall founded and presided over the Southern California Alumni Association, which served as the inspiration of educational life for the black community. She also participated in other religious, fraternal, and secular organizations, all dedicated to racial uplift. Another prominent clubwoman in Los Angeles, Eva Carter Buckner, often published essays about the black community in both the *Los Angeles Times* and the *California Eagle*. Black Angeleno women also organized local branches of the Harriet Tubman Red Cross Auxiliary, the African American branch of the Young Women's Christian Association (YWCA), the NAACP, the Women's Auxiliary of the Colored Voters League, the Sons and Daughters of Africa, and the Young Women's Married Thimble Club, as well as other clubs geared toward uniting people from particular regions of the country. The club movement became such an integral part of black women's lives in Los Angeles that national African American women's club leader and wife of Booker T. Washington, Margaret Washington, was invited to speak at the state women's club federation, and petition the national organization to integrate its movement in 1906.[30]

The African American community also used its clubs and churches for political organizing, and for forming new institutions. The Los Angeles chapter of the NAACP (1913), for example, was one of the main political organizations aimed at maintaining equality for African Americans. By the beginning of the twentieth century, with increasing numbers of African American migrants, racism and segregation became more significant. Some black Angelenos such as John Somerville remained active in the NAACP and kept in close contact with W.E.B. Du Bois long after he left California.[31] In addition to the local NAACP, other organizations sought racial equality.

In 1902, the Los Angeles Forum organized around Booker T. Washington's premise of self-help. This club assisted new migrants transition into Los Angeles culture and society. Some African Americans also joined the United Negro Improvement Association (UNIA) organized in 1921, and was headed by Charlotta Bass. Some clubs acted independently, while others represented local branches of national organizations. Regardless, black Angelenos, especially women, created an outlet to combat racism and discrimination.[32] Each of these clubs focused on improving conditions of the African American community.[33]

Although some clubs and organizations had social agendas, politics remained a priority. While members organized socials, teas, balls, and charity events, they never strayed from the current political conflicts. This proved especially true during height of the Progressive era, when predominantly middle class values of social reform were a central theme nationwide. Some groups focused on issues such as mental illness, alcohol consumption, and other forms of moral reform. Others took a stance against discrimination and racism, and attempted to address social issues involving the African American community.[34] An example of this was the position the *California Eagle* took against D. W. Griffith's 1915 film, "The Birth of a Nation," Hollywood's first major motion picture. The film glorified the Ku Klux Klan and justified extreme violence against African Americans by suggesting that emancipation was a mistake, and projected images of black men sexually pursuing white women, suggesting they needed to be controlled.

The *Eagle* called on local "civic, political, and religious organizations" to help stop the production of the film.[35] Bass wanted to boycott the film but she felt conflicted, recognizing that doing so would jeopardize people's livelihoods. The film company employed several black Angeleno actors and crewmembers. Bass and her staff understood the economic opportunity, and did not want to force people out of work. She later noted that the paper did make small gains, by "forcing Griffith to cut some of the most vicious attacks against the morals of the Negro people which had been in the early rushes, in the early reels, of the production."[36] In retrospect, however, Bass said, "the film did disturb the peace, did create not understanding and cooperation but hatred and fear of one group by the other."[37] She was proud that the *Eagle* had led the charge against racism and hatred.

Under Bass's leadership, the *Eagle* turned its attention to politics, focusing on national elections. Women in California were granted the right to vote in 1911, and Charlotta Bass used her newspaper to make sure all black Angelenos participated in the political process. The *Eagle* organized meetings to address political party affiliation, since the majority of black voters were Republican. Bass wanted black voters to really think about which political party had the black community's best interest in mind. She also saw that African Americans would make up a strong voting bloc not just in local, but in national politics as well. African American political aspirations proved fruitful. The hard work and organizing of black women during the nineteenth century made it possible for black Angelenos to combat racism and gender discrimination effectively in the twentieth century.[38]

In the decades after California became a state, African American women worked tirelessly to advance themselves, their families, and the community being formed in Los Angeles. Similar to the social activism among African American women in eastern and midwestern cities, they fought for the full freedom of people oppressed first by the institution of slavery and then by its echoes. They raised funds to support local civil rights litigation and organized to improve educational opportunities for children and adults. Although women were excluded from most political organizations in the nineteenth century, their fundraising activities supported civil rights campaigns and touched the social and economic lives of African American men, women, and children making Los Angeles their home.[39] As economic opportunities became available, and black migration to Los Angeles increased, so did the number of African Americans achieving the American dream of home ownership.

Property Acquisition

Of the 532 black household heads listed in 1900, just fewer than 30 percent owned property, either farms or homes, while an additional 70 percent rented. A few household heads did not have information listed in terms of property ownership. Most people lived in small, modest bungalows consisting of a moderately sized living room, a dining area, a small kitchen, two bedrooms, and a bathroom. Many of the homes had medium-sized back yards, and a porch in front. Wealthier black Angelenos lived in much more spacious houses on large lots, typically in the larger Craftsman or Victorian style of architecture. Only one man, George Palmer, a 41-year-old farmer from New York owned his farm outright, while two others, a 32-year-old brickyard laborer from Texas, and junk dealer Allen Fontane (23) who came from Louisiana, paid mortgages. Of the homeowners, 75 were paying mortgages compared to 69 who owned them outright. In all, 151 people reported that they owned their property, while 373 rented. One woman, Mary Fairfield, a 49-year-old widowed

Table 3.7 African American property ownership by gender, 1900

	Men	Women	Gender Unknown	Total
House	6	2		8
Own	1			1
Own Farm Free	1			1
Own Farm Mortgage	2			2
Own House	5			5
Own House Free	60	7		67
Own House Mortgage	68	7		75
Rent	4		1	5
Rent Farm	0	1		1
Rent House	207	75		282
No Information	69	14	2	85
	423	**106**	**3**	**532**

Source: 1900 U.S. Federal Census

white mother of a "mulatto" son rented a farm. Table 3.7 shows the range of black and interracial family property acquisition by 1900. Eight people reported that they lived in a house but no information about ownership status was given. One listed ownership, but no indication as to whether he owned a farm, house, or paid a mortgage.[40]

Although some people are difficult to trace from 1870 to 1910, several of the founding community members or their descendants do stand out. Hannah Embers's grandson, Manuel Pepper, for instance, was only seven years old in 1870, living with his parents, Manuel (Sr.) and Ann, and his four other siblings. By 1900, he owned his own home on South Fourth Street where he cared for his mother and youngest sister. Their family, just like Biddy Mason's, is one of the few that can be traced into the twentieth century.[41]

By 1910, the amount of African American households had increased, and there were more property owners. Out of 1,980 household heads in the black community, approximately 38 percent owned property, while 60 percent rented. 293 household heads owned their homes completely, while an additional 408 people had mortgages. A small number of household heads (2 percent) did not identify their status. No household heads

Table 3.8 African American property ownership by gender, 1910

	Female	Male	Total
House	11	24	35
Own House Free	56	237	293
Own House	2	6	8
Own House Mortgage	55	353	408
Own Mortgage Farm	0	3	3
Rent	0	1	1
Rent Farm	0	1	1
Rent Farm House	0	1	1
Rent House	288	897	1185
Unknown	11	34	45
Total	**423**	**1557**	**1980**

Source: 1910 U.S. Federal Census

reported owning farms free and clear, while two people rented farms, and three mortgaged theirs. Almost 1,200 people rented (table 3.8). A noticeable difference from northern or southern cities is evidenced in property ownership. Regardless of one's occupation, property acquisition seemed possible. Richard Hart, a 61-year-old cook, for example, migrated from Arkansas to Los Angeles, and purchased his home in full on Woodward Avenue. Charles Perry was on his second marriage at the age of forty-seven. He was plasterer, doing cement work, and he owned his home outright, where he lived with his wife, Birdie, a 31-year-old woman from Tennessee, his three stepsons, Eddie (15) who worked as a driver, hauling things, Henry (13), and William (10). While Birdie and Charles were both listed as black, all three of her sons were listed as "mulatto." The couple also had two sons together—a 2-year-old named Charles, and a 3-month-old named Nathaniel. They were both listed as black. Cylas Vena was an 81-year-old from Kentucky who lived with his daughter, Sina (37) after losing his wife. He worked as a janitor for city hall. He also owned his home on Bonnie Brae Street outright.[42]

In 1910, the role of household head was not universally restricted by gender, although the majority was male. Women made up 21 percent of black household heads, and were either widowed or divorced, with children or renters living with them. Catherine Wildberger, a 68-year-old woman from Alabama, owned her home free and clear of debt, which

she lived in with her 38-year-old daughter, Ruth Ann Neworth. Catherine did not report any employment in 1910, but Ruth Ann worked as a
servant for a family. Ophelia Sparks was a widow from Tennessee. She
lived on Council Street where she owned her home outright. She earned
money by washing clothes in her home, and she rented a room to an el-
derly man named Peter Hollands (70). He cooked for a private family.
His grandson, Oli and his wife also lived in the home. Oli worked in a
restaurant as a waiter, and Blanche was a domestic servant. Both were
twenty-three years old. Harriet Parker (65) was widowed and also took
in laundry for a living. She lived alone. Men, on the other hand, usually
lived with their nuclear family units.[43]

Only 425 of the black property owners were women compared to
1,555 men. On the other hand, 1198 men rented, as opposed 290 female
household heads. Renters' households mirrored that of owners', mean-
ing that regardless of whether they owned property, women were more
likely to be widowed, divorced, or living in households with boarders
or extended family members, possibly along with their children, while
male household heads who rented were likely to live with their nuclear
families. A closer look at household size from 1880 to 1910 lends to a better
understanding of African American community formation over time.[44]

Household Analysis

Household sizes in 1880 were small. The African American community
in Los Angeles in 1880 comprised 103 people. There were only three more
households than 1870, totaling twenty-eight, with eight female household
heads, along with twenty male. Of the twenty, two white household heads
were married to "mulatto" women. Thirteen people identified themselves as non-household heads, living in someone else's home. An additional five worked for the railroad, and two more were listed as boarders.
The number of household heads made up 27 percent of the total African
American population of Los Angeles. Female heads tended to be older,
averaging 46½ years of age, compared to 38 years for men.[45]

Household sizes tended to be small, averaging 2.5 people for male-
headed households, and only one for women. Table 3.9 illustrates these
trends. The largest households included eight for men and six for women.
The Cook family was the largest amongst African Americans that census
year. Belt Cook was a 36-year-old barber from Maryland, and his 33-year-
old wife Rebecca kept house. His entire family was listed as "mulatto" in

Figure 3.1 Family portrait, Los Angeles ca. 1918. Although it was not the norm, it was not uncommon for women to head their own household. Los Angeles Public Library. Security National Bank Collection.

1880. The couple had three sons, John (14), Charles (10), and Elias (7), who all attended school, while their three daughters, Eva (13), May (12), and Hattie (2) did not.[46]

Women represented eight out of the twenty-eight household heads. Similar to previous decades, these households were small. Of the eight, the largest female-headed household was comprised of six members. Ann Daniels, the eldest daughter of Hannah Embers, had the largest female-headed household. The 37-year-old woman was raising her neighbor's stepdaughter, Jane (7), along with her own son Henry (8), and her two sons, Manuel (17) and Louis (18) Pepper. As in 1870, female household heads tended to be older, with forty-seven being the average age of women and thirty-eight for men. There was a bit more occupational difference from the previous decade.[47] Sarah Smart was a 48-year-old woman from Arkansas, and kept her own house while her two eldest children, William (21) was a janitor and Clarissa (18) worked as a cook. Her three youngest children, Leonora (16), John (8), and Margaret (6) attended school.

Table 3.9 African American household size, 1880

Members	Female	Male	Total
1	3	2	5
2	2	10	12
3	1	2	3
4	0	4	4
5	0	1	1
6	2	0	2
7	0	0	0
8	0	1	1
9	0	0	0
10	0	0	0
Total	**8**	**20**	**28**

Source: 1880 U.S. Federal Census

Table 3.10 African American household size, 1900

Household Size	Men	Women	Gender Unknown	Total
1	59	35		94
2	95	27		122
3	92	23	2	117
4	49	9	1	59
5	54	4		58
6	33	1		34
7	23	1		24
8	14	2		16
9	1	2		3
10	2	0		2
11	3	0		3
Total	**425**	**104**	**3**	**532**

Source: 1900 U.S. Federal Census

Table 3.11 African American household size, 1910

Household Size	Male	Female	Amount	Percent
1	107	112	219	11.1%
2	487	122	609	30.76%
3	322	68	390	19.7%
4	261	50	311	15.71%
5	141	29	170	8.6%
6	102	19	121	6.11%
7	65	11	76	3.8%
8	33	7	40	2.02%
9	19	4	23	1.2%
10	9	0	9	0.5%
11	2	2	4	0.20%
12	4	1	5	0.3%
13	2	0	2	0.10%
15	1	0	1	0.1%
Total	**1555**	**425**	**1980**	**100.00%**

Source: 1910 U.S. Federal Census

Men also maintained small households. Fourteen (70 percent) of the twenty were made up of three or fewer members. Five households were comprised of four or five members.[48] While the African American population remained small between 1870 and 1880, rapid increases occurred over the next two decades, but that made little impact on household structure or size (see table 3.10).[49]

The average black household in 1900 comprised three people. Male-headed households averaged about one more person than female households (3.6 people versus 2.5). Women made up 20 percent of total black household heads (106), while men accounted for 80 percent (423). There were three household heads listed but no information about their gender was recorded in the census.[50]

Household characteristics the next decade strayed very little from previous years. In 1910, families remained small (table 3.11), averaging less than four people per household (3.39). Although some households were large, they were exceptional. These usually included extended family members, boarders, or a combination of both. The average age for female heads of households was 44, while males were slightly younger (41).

Figure 3.2 African American couple. Los Angeles Public Library. Security Pacific National Bank Collection.

John Neimore, editor of the *California Eagle*, for example, lived with his wife, Ida, daughter, Bessie, and two roomers, Daniel Hodge and Oscar Wilson, both of whom came to Los Angeles from Texas, Neimore's place of birth. Julius and Nannie Loving rented rooms to nine men. Henderson Benjamin and his wide Ida lived with their four small children, all under 11 years of age, as well as Henderson's brother and sister-in-law and two borders. John and Irene Lockridge lived with their 8-year-old daughter and rented rooms to a family of three, the Flemmings. Susan Flemming was a 50-year-old laundress who was widowed, and had two school-aged children, Ruth (16) and Leroy (10). The family also rented a room to a 97-year-old widow named Jane William.[51]

By 1910, men sustained slightly larger households than women. The average size for male-headed households equaled 3.54 people. Female-headed households, on the other hand, contained approximately 2.88 members, and there were proportionally more of them than the previous decade (21%). Men made up 79 percent of the total household heads. Less than 1.5% of all households comprised ten to fifteen members. While